CONTENTS

KU-646-945

Introduction

The Wealth Divide is the fifty-sixth volume in the **Issues** series. The aim of this series is to offer up-to-date information about important issues in our world.

The Wealth Divide examines poverty in the UK and around the world.

The information comes from a wide variety of sources and includes:
Government reports and statistics
Newspaper reports and features
Magazine articles and surveys
Web site material
Literature from lobby groups
and charitable organisations.

It is hoped that, as you read about the many aspects of the issues explored in this book, you will critically evaluate the information presented. It is important that you decide whether you are being presented with facts or opinions. Does the writer give a biased or an unbiased report? If an opinion is being expressed, do you agree with the writer?

The Wealth Divide offers a useful starting-point for those who need convenient access to information about the many issues involved. However, it is only a starting-point. At the back of the book is a list of organisations which you may want to contact for further information.

*****

About poverty in the UK

Information from Oxfam

It is certainly true that Britain, as a wealthy country, does not face the problem of absolute poverty on the endemic scale found in many countries where Oxfam works, but this does not mean that Britain is a society without poverty and inequality.

Oxfam believes that poverty is more than just a lack of the resources needed for basic survival. It is also a state of powerlessness, where people are excluded from society and find themselves powerless, unable to make any change for the better in their lives, and unable to live a life that would be considered reasonable for their society. Although the scale and intensity of poverty varies from country to country, the damage it does to people in terms of deprivation and social exclusion is similar everywhere.

No UK government has ever agreed an official definition of poverty, though the government does compile measurements of low incomes in the UK. According to the latest Households Below Average Income statistics, in 1994/5 22% of the population of the UK were living on or below half of the average income (an increase from 9% in 1979). This includes nearly one in three British children.

People who find themselves living on a low income, through unemployment or low pay, are vulnerable to many problems associated with their poverty. A report by the Family Budget Unit estimated that the cost of a modest but adequate diet for a family of four comes to £69 a week. If that family were living on income support, the amount of money they would have for food in their weekly budget would be just £41. It is no wonder that many families find themselves unable to make ends meet and parents often have to go hungry to ensure their children are fed.

Malnutrition is becoming an ever-greater problem among those on low incomes, and health workers are again reporting cases of stunted growth in children, as well as incidences of rickets and tuberculosis, diseases which most people would associate with the poverty of Victorian times. This ill health perpetuates a vicious circle, often making it virtually impossible for people to lift themselves out of the poverty trap. Inadequate housing and lack of money for heating also account for many health problems, especially amongst children and the elderly.

It is now generally accepted (even by the World Bank) that the 'trickle down' theory of economic growth is a fallacy. As in other countries where Oxfam works, many of the benefits of growth are bypassing large sections of the community. A recent survey concluded that Britain is the most unequal country in the developed world after New Zealand, with a wealth gap between the richest and poorest in society wider than in Ethiopia or Ghana. Since 1979, the richest 10% of the British population have seen their income rise by 65% in real terms, whilst the income of the poorest 10% has actually dropped by 13%.

High levels of inequality are harmful to the whole of society, not just those on the lowest incomes. The result is a breakdown of social cohesion, and can mean an increase in many social problems. A return to a more equal society would benefit everyone in Britain, not just those who are currently the worst-off.

Oxfam believes that poverty is not inevitable. It is caused by human decisions and actions. Poverty can and must be tackled, to change society and people's lives for the better.

■ The above information is from Oxfam's web site which can be found at www.oxfam.org.uk

© Oxfam

Poverty key facts

Information from the New Policy Institute

Income

- The most commonly used threshold of low incomes is 60% of median income after deducting housing costs. In 2000/01, this equated to £176 per week for a couple with no children, £107 for a single person, £257 for a couple with two children and £188 for a lone parent with two children.
- In 2000/01, 13 million people were living on incomes below this income threshold. This represents a drop of 1 million since 1996/97.
- The numbers of people on relative low incomes remained broadly unchanged during the 1990s after having doubled in the 1980s.
- In 2000/01, there were 9 million people on incomes below the fixed threshold of 60% of 1994/95 median income. This represents a drop of around 4 million since 1996/97.

Child poverty

- The number of children living in households below 60% of median income was 4 million in 2000/01.
- This represents a drop of $\frac{1}{2}$ million since 1996/97.
- Children are one and a half times more likely to live in a low income household than adults.
- 2 million children live in workless households.

Work

- In 2001, there were $3\frac{1}{2}$ million people who wanted to be in paid work but were not, compared to 5 million at its peak in 1993. This rate of reduction is much less than the rate of reduction in ILO unemployment because the numbers who are 'economically inactive but would like work' have remained unchanged.
- The number of long-term workless households has been consistently above 2 million since 1995 and shows no signs of falling.

- Nearly a half of all lone parents do not have paid work.
- Around $\frac{1}{2}$ million young adults aged 16 to 24 were unemployed in 2001 (around 10%). Numbers have halved since their peak in 1993 but young adult unemployment rates are still twice those for older workers.
- $1\frac{1}{2}$ million people were on temporary contracts in 2001, unchanged from five years previously.
- People without qualifications are three times less likely to receive job-related training compared with those with some qualifications.

Low pay

- $1\frac{1}{2}$ million adults aged 22 to retirement were paid below half male median hourly pay in 2000, compared to 2 million in 1998 (when the national minimum wage was introduced).

People without qualifications are three times less likely to receive job-related training compared with those with some qualifications

---

- $\frac{1}{2}$ million young adults aged 18 to 21 were paid less than half the male median hourly income in 2000, unchanged since 1998.

Education

- 11-year-olds: The proportion failing to achieve level 4 or above at key stage 2 in English and Maths fell by 40% during the 1990s but children in schools with relatively high numbers on free school meals continue to do much worse than other schools.
- 16-year-olds: In 1999/2000, around 150,000 pupils (25%) got no grades above a D at GCSE, 20% less than a decade previously. 25,000 (4%) got no grades at all.
- 19-year-olds: 200,000 had no basic qualifications (without an NVQ2 or equivalent) in 2001, compared to 300,000 in 1992.
- 10,000 pupils were permanently excluded from school in 2000/01. This represents a fall of a quarter since their peak in 1996/97.

Health

- After rising throughout most of the last decade, geographic concentrations of premature deaths fell in 2000. Scotland has by far the highest proportion of premature deaths for men: a third of its local authorities had high male mortality rates compared to one in ten for Great Britain as a whole.
- People on below-average incomes are twice as likely to develop a mental illness than those on average and higher incomes.
- Levels of long-standing illness or disability remained unchanged during the 1990s and unskilled manual workers are $1\frac{1}{2}$ times as likely to have a long-standing illness or disability than professional classes.
- The number of accidental deaths of children has halved over the last decade but children from

The proportion of elderly people aged 75 and over who receive support from social services to help them live at home is now two-thirds of what it was at the peak in 1994

manual social classes are still 1½ times more likely to die in accidents than children from non-manual social classes.

- The proportion of babies who are of low birthweight has not changed over the last five years and children from manual social classes are one and a third times more likely to be born underweight than children from non-manual social classes.

- The number of births to girls conceiving before their 16th birthday has fallen by 20% since its peak in 1996, but the vast majority of these births are concentrated in the manual social classes.

- 600 young adults aged 15 to 24 committed suicide in 2000, down by a fifth from a decade earlier. But young men in the manual social classes are still twice as likely to commit suicide as those in the non-manual classes.

Crime

- On the latest British Crime Survey statistics (1999), the number of burglaries was at its lowest level for a decade. But lone parents and households headed by young people are three times more likely to be burgled than the average.

- Households with no household insurance are around three times as likely to be burgled as those with insurance. Half of those on low income do not have any household insurance – compared with a fifth for households on average income.

- People in low income households are twice as likely to report that their quality of

life is significantly affected by fear of crime than the average and almost twice as likely to feel very dissatisfied with the area in which they live.

Housing

- People in low income households are twice as likely to report that their quality of life is significantly affected by fear of crime than the average and almost twice as likely to feel very dissatisfied with the area in which they live.

- Levels of overcrowding have almost halved in the last decade, but overcrowding in the social rented sector is now three times the level than for those with mortgages and has not reduced over the decade.

- The number of low income households without central heating has reduced by a third since 1994/95, but households in the private rented sector are twice as likely as other households to be without central heating

- Families with expectant mothers and dependent children constitute two-thirds of households considered to be in priority housing need in England.

Ethnic minorities

- People of Black Caribbean, Pakistani, Bangladeshi and African ethnicity are around twice as likely to be out of work and wanting work compared with white people.

- Although the rate of permanent

exclusions for black pupils fell by a fifth between 1998/99 and 1999/2000, they were still four times more likely to be excluded than whites.

- Black young adults are seven times as likely as white young adults to be in prison.

- Asians are three times more likely to report that their quality of life is greatly affected by the fear of crime than people on average.

- Bangladeshis and Pakistanis are twice as likely not to have a bank or building society account than the rest of the population.

Older people

- In 1999/2000, 1¼ million pensioners had no income other than the state pension, unchanged from a decade previously.

- 15% of pensioner couples aged 75 and under are in the poorest fifth of the population compared to 22% of other pensioners.

- The proportion of elderly people aged 75 and over who receive support from social services to help them live at home is now two-thirds of what it was at the peak in 1994. County councils and unitary authorities appear to support far fewer households than either urban or Welsh authorities

Communities

- The poorest fifth of the population are 1½ times less likely to participate in any social, political, cultural or community organisation than the richest fifth.

- In two-thirds of households in social housing, the head of the household is not in paid work. In three-quarters, the head of the household has a gross weekly income of less than £200.

- A fifth of the poorest households did not have any type of bank / building society account in 2000/01, largely unchanged from 5 years previously.

■ The above information is from the web site www.poverty.org.uk Alternatively, see page 41 for their address details.

© *New Policy Institute*

New website uncovers picture of UK poverty

By David Batty

The New Policy Institute think-tank has launched a website that provides a comprehensive breakdown of poverty and social deprivation levels in the UK.

Set up with the Joseph Rowntree Foundation, 'Monitoring Poverty and Social Exclusion' contains in-depth evaluation of social exclusion, covering factors such as income, employment, health, housing, education and crime.

The site, launched yesterday, is based on the monitoring poverty and social exclusion reports issued annually by the institute and foundation since 1998, but it also offers graphs and statistics and analyses trends over the past 10 years.

It includes a new examination of how and why poverty rates have changed under New Labour.

Headline figures showed that the number of people in households with below 60% of average income after housing costs, the most commonly used low income threshold, fell from 14 million to 13 million between 1996-97 and 2000-01. The number of children in low income households fell by 500,000 over the same period.

The research by the two think-tanks shows that the main reason for these falls was that more people were in work in 2001 than in 1997. But it reveals that employment does not guarantee an escape from poverty. Apart from pensioners, almost half of all adults and children below the low income threshold were living in households where at least one adult had a job.

The research also shows that while the breadth of poverty declined – gauged by the number of people below the threshold – there was no reduction in the depth of poverty, exposing how far income falls short of the average.

Peter Kenway, co-director of the institute, said, 'The government's anti-poverty strategy rests on the idea that employment should be the way out of poverty for all those who can work.

'These figures show that for millions work is not yet providing an escape from poverty.'

Fellow co-director Guy Palmer added: 'It is vital that the poverty debate is driven by an understanding of what has actually been happening rather than by soundbite and prejudice. Our new website and associated analyses will help achieve this.'

The government was strongly criticised by poverty campaigners in April after announcing plans to redefine child poverty, only a week after it was forced to admit it had failed to lift 1.2 million people out of relative poverty in the first parliament, a key Labour manifesto claim.

■ Visit the web site at www.poverty.org.uk/intro/index.htm

Poverty key facts

Poverty

- 4.1 million children are living in poverty in the UK
- The proportion of children who are living in poverty has grown from 1 in 10 in 1979 to 1 in 3 in 1998.
- The UK has one of the worst rates of child poverty in the industrialised world
- Risks are highest for children living in families without a working parent
  - lone parent families
  - families with young mothers (aged 16-24)
  - minority ethnic families
  - families with 3 or more children
  - families containing one or more disabled persons, either a child or an adult

The effects

- 1 in 3 poor children do not have three meals a day
- 1 in 3 poor children miss out on toys, school trips and out-of-school activities
- 1 in 3 poor children lack adequate clothing, particularly shoes and winter coats
- Poverty in childhood increases the likelihood of unemployment and low income in adulthood
- In 1993/5 the infant mortality rate for social class 5 was 70% higher than the rate for social class 1
- Children aged up to 14 from unskilled families are 5 times more likely to die in an accident than children from professional families, and 15 times more likely to die in a fire at home.

■ The above information is from the End Child Poverty Coalition's web site which can be found at www.ecpc.org.uk

What is child poverty?

Information from Save the Children

Consultations with children and adults world-wide show that poverty has many faces. As well as not having enough money, poverty can mean being unable to control your life, being vulnerable to the will of more powerful people, having to demean yourself to make ends meet, not being able to take a full part in community life, and feeling inferior to other people around you. It also means not having enough to eat, inadequate shelter, poor health and no education.

The causes of poverty include conflict, natural disasters, population growth, poor governance, limited employment opportunities or access to land, failed economic strategies and social and economic inequality brought about by disability, ethnicity, age or gender.

How we understand both the nature and causes of poverty is fundamental to our ability to find solutions.

Child poverty is where children grow up:

- In households with inadequate resources to provide for their material needs.
- Where families and communities are unable to nurture and protect them.
- Unable to develop their full potential and are, for example, uneducated or ill.

Poverty exists in both the North and the South. While poor people in Britain are not as materially poor as people in the South, their poverty is certainly real. It exists in lack of access to what is generally regarded as a reasonable standard and quality of life in the UK. It is also a state of powerlessness, whereby people are excluded from society and find themselves unable to make any change for the better in their lives.

Why is child poverty important?

Child poverty is a potential time

Save the Children

bomb, and tackling it is an urgent development priority. As one of the most powerless groups in society, children often bear the heaviest burden. Children are as much if not more affected than adults as the costs of family poverty are often passed on to them through poor diet, inadequate time to mature or the ill effects of alcoholism and depression.

How we understand both the nature and causes of poverty is fundamental to our ability to find solutions

---

Childhood is a one-off window of development, which makes investing in children a priority and not a choice. Damage at this stage cannot often be overcome later in life. The consequences of allowing poverty and failing to invest in children go beyond individuals to affect the health, well-being and productivity of society as a whole.

In many of the world's poorest countries children under the age of 15 make up over 40 per cent of the population. The highest proportions are Palestine (52 per cent), Uganda (50 per cent), Angola (48 per cent), Somalia (48 per cent), Congo (48 per cent) and Burundi (47 per cent). Even in the UK, young people under 15 make up 19 per cent of the population.

■ The above information is an extract from *What is Child Poverty? – Facts, Measurements and Conclusions*. Printed with kind permission of Save the Children

© The Save the Child Fund

The child poverty league

The table shows the percentage of children living in 'relative' poverty, defined as households with income below 50 per cent of the national median.

Country	Percentage
Sweden	2.6
Norway	3.9
Finland	4.3
Belgium	4.4
Luxembourg	4.5
Denmark	5.1
Czech Republic	5.9
Netherlands	7.7
France	7.9
Hungary	10.3
Germany	10.7
Japan	12.2
Spain	12.3
Greece	12.3
Australia	12.6
Poland	15.4
Canada	15.5
Ireland	16.8
Turkey	19.7
UK	19.8
Italy	20.5
USA	22.4
Mexico	26.2

Source: Child Poverty in Rich Nations, UNICEF

Child poverty indicators

The government plans to redefine poverty. David Batty examines the possible changes

How many children live in poverty?
The latest figures from the office of national statistics (ONS) show that last year there were 3.9 million children living in poverty in Britain – a reduction of 500,000 since 1997. The government has pledged to halve child poverty by 2010 and eradicate it by 2020.

How does this compare with other countries?
Mike Aaronson, director general of charity Save the Children, said even if the government meets its 10-year target this would still leave the UK with the highest child poverty rate in Europe.

How do we measure child poverty?
New Labour has defined child poverty as any child living in a household with below 60% of average income after housing. However, following the former Department of Social Security report *Opportunity for All* (1999), which set out the government's strategy to tackle poverty and social exclusion, progress on tackling child poverty has been tracked against 15 indicators. These include the number of children in unemployed families, educational achievement, truancy, health inequalities, child abuse, teenage pregnancy and housing standards.

What alternatives are proposed?
A consultation paper issued by the Department for Work and Pensions (DWP) set out four options. The first would use a small number of indicators to track low income, unemployment, education, health and housing. The second involves constructing an index that combines a small number of indicators to produce a final headline figure to track progress. The third would use a headline measure of 'consistent poverty', which combines relative low income and material deprivation. The forth uses a set of core indicators

of low income and consistent poverty.

Why should the definition be changed?
The DWP paper contends that it is far from straightforward to measure poverty. The influential centre-left thinktank the Institute for Public Policy Research (IPPR), which has been advising the government on setting a new measurement, believes that the current definition is arbitrary and hard for the public to grasp. Lisa Harker, IPPR deputy director, said: 'There's a need to convince the public that poverty needs to be tackled. But it's difficult for people to conceptualise what the 60% figure means.' She supports the third option outlined in measuring child poverty. This would combine a relative

Holidays

Children in households unable to afford a week's holiday away from home

Netherlands	14%
Germany	18%
Luxembourg	21%
Denmark	23%
Belgium	27%
France	34%
Italy	36%
Greece	47%
UK	47%
Spain	52%
Ireland	53%
Portugal	62%

Source: Child Poverty in Rich Nations, UNICEF

measure of income and whether people can afford 'essentials', such as a warm overcoat, a new pair of shoes or two hot meals a week.

Why is this controversial?
Child poverty campaigners argue that the government is shifting the goalposts because the ONS revealed it has failed to meet chancellor Gordon Brown's boast of reducing the number of children living in poverty by 1.2 million since coming to power. Dr Peter Kenway, director of thinktank the New Policy Institute, said the number of people on relative low income had become established as the indicator of progress on poverty in the UK. 'It is a simple and reliable statistic, which has played a huge part in propelling poverty high up the political agenda,' he said. 'Downgrading or obscuring it will be met with great cynicism and taken as a sign that the government is going soft on poverty.'

How might a new definition change poverty rates?
The Irish government set out its first official definition of poverty in the 1997 national anti-poverty strategy. This incorporated the number of people with below 60% of average income and material deprivation – in line with the definition of consistent poverty outlined in option three of the DWP consultation paper. Before this the measure was usually based on the number of people on below 50% of average income. In 2000, 26% of the Irish population were classified as poor under the relative income measure, whereas only 6% were under the new definition. According to the IPPR, the consistent poverty measure was set because although average income rose in the 1990s so did the relative number of those in poverty, even though overall standards of living had improved.

© *Guardian Newspapers Limited 2002*

Poverty and social exclusion

Information from NCH

Problems of definition and measurement

Poverty is usually taken to refer to a lack of material resources, in particular, income. Social exclusion, on the other hand, generally connotes an inability to participate effectively in economic, social, political and cultural life, so that the people affected are unable to enjoy the activities or take advantage of the opportunities that others take for granted.

There are two main approaches to measuring poverty. One sees poverty in *absolute* terms and tends to emphasis basic physical needs and discount social and cultural norms. The other sees poverty *relatively*, in terms of generally accepted standards of living in a particular society. There is no official measure of poverty. However, the one that is most frequently used, if not universally accepted, the UK and across the EU, is 50% of average income. People whose incomes are below this line are than defined as (relatively) poor. Some people criticise this, with some justification, on the basis that it is a measure of *inequality* rather than poverty.

The question of how best to measure poverty has become much more urgent since 1997, when the Government announced its intention to end child poverty by 2019, with intermediate targets to halve it by 2010 and reduce it to a quarter by 2004. The Government has made a start by setting out a number of indicators to help it to measures progress. These include health and education outcomes that relate to social exclusion, as well as measure of poverty such as a reduction in the proportion of children in households with persistently low incomes. The Government has chosen 60% of median income as its 'poverty line'.

However, the Government has not yet produced a single definition of 'child poverty' against which its ultimate aim of eradicating it can be judged. Academics, campaigners and Government officials are all working on this at time of writing. The challenge is to develop a measure that is meaningful, simple, transparent and – from the Government's point of view, especially – achievable. An added difficulty is posed by the time lags inherent in the process of measuring change in incomes, meaning that even if progress is being made, it takes a long time to show.

Framing targets purely in terms of relative incomes may seem initially attractive but the problem with this approach is that very limited or no progress may be registered in a period when average incomes are rising rapidly, even if deprivation levels for poor people are declining significantly. Moreover, arriving at a situation where no, or very few, households with children report incomes below 60% of the median would be an extremely ambitious target, not currently attained even in the best-performing welfare states.

Therefore, attention is now focusing on more sophisticated means of measuring child poverty that combine relative income measures with non-monetary ways of tracking deprivation, which are better able to monitor exclusion. (To this end the Department for Work and Pensions produced a consultation paper on measuring child poverty in April 2002.) Ireland already has a model of this kind.

Sources: *Opportunity for all: tackling poverty and social exclusion, the third annual report*, DWP, The Stationery Office, 2001; 'Moving targets: measuring and targeting child poverty' by Nolan B., Economic and Social Research Institute, Dublin, in *New Economy*, IPPR 2001; *Measuring child poverty*, DWP, The Stationery Office, 2002.

■ The above information is an extract from *Factfile 2002-03* produced by NCH and available from NCH's Supporter Helpline on 0845 762 6579 priced at £8.50.

© NCH

Poor measures?

Information from the Social Market Foundation

By Tom Startup

- The Government's conventional measure of poverty – those living on less than 60% of median income – is flawed since it is a crude measure of inequality, not poverty.
- There is good evidence that the median income measure of poverty is failing to accurately identify those who are experiencing poverty.
- The Government urgently needs to settle on a better measure of poverty if it is to be able to assess the effectiveness of its policies in tackling poverty.
- Any good measure of poverty must satisfy the requirements of being simple, intuitive, consistent, useful, robust, objective, appropriately relative and comparable.
- Measures used by international organisations and other nations do not offer a measure that would be adequate as a headline measure of poverty in the UK.
- The measures used by the UN and World Bank are crude measures of 'absolute' income poverty and low-level deprivation and as such are insufficiently tailored to the specific living conditions typical in the UK. They are not intuitive, useful, or appropriately relative.
- The US model is based on a sound principle – that a poverty line can be defined by establishing how much income a family needs to be able to afford an acceptable standard of living. However, the measure is not appropriately sensitive to changes in the pattern of household expenditure, to increases in the standard of living over time, or to variations in household costs. It also fails because it is not intuitive, useful, or appropriately relative.
- The Irish model of 'consistent poverty' is flawed for three reasons. First, it does not capture those who have inadequate material resources since it retains the median income measure. Second, there is little rationale for adopting as the primary measure those who experience both low incomes and deprivation since the experience of deprivation is time-lagged with respect to the possession of a low income. Last, there are methodological difficulties with assessing enforced deprivation by asking respondents which items they 'want but cannot afford'.
- The best measure of poverty – termed the 'Basic Household Costs' (BHC) approach – involves the budget standards methodology which establishes a poverty line by determining how much money families need in order to be able to achieve an acceptable standard of living. This measure best fulfils the requirements of being simple, intuitive, consistent, useful, robust, objective, appropriately relative and comparable.
- The BHC measure can usefully be supplemented by measures of deprivation which help both to check that the poverty line is set in the right place and to better inform policy-makers about the relationship between poverty and deprivation. The measure supplemented in this way is referred to as BHC+.
- The effect on the poverty rate of adopting the BHC+ measure is uncertain although there is evidence that the poverty line for a BHC approach is likely to be higher for working lone parents than that given by the median income measure of poverty.

- The Government's high profile commitment to eradicate poverty in Britain is bound to fail because of its flawed definition of the problem, argues the SMF's latest pamphlet, *Poor Measures?*, published on 27 August 2002 of which this information is the executive summary.

- To order a copy of *Poor Measures?*, please call 020 7222 7060 or e-mail info@smf.co.uk. Price £10. Alternatively visit the Social Market Foundation's web site at www.smf.co.uk

© *Social Market Foundation*

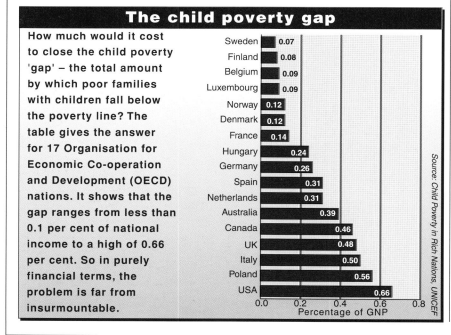

The child poverty gap

How much would it cost to close the child poverty 'gap' – the total amount by which poor families with children fall below the poverty line? The table gives the answer for 17 Organisation for Economic Co-operation and Development (OECD) nations. It shows that the gap ranges from less than 0.1 per cent of national income to a high of 0.66 per cent. So in purely financial terms, the problem is far from insurmountable.

Country	Percentage of GNP
Sweden	0.07
Finland	0.08
Belgium	0.09
Luxembourg	0.09
Norway	0.12
Denmark	0.12
France	0.14
Hungary	0.24
Germany	0.26
Spain	0.31
Netherlands	0.31
Australia	0.39
Canada	0.46
UK	0.48
Italy	0.50
Poland	0.56
USA	0.66

Source: Child Poverty in Rich Nations, UNICEF

Listening to children

Their contribution to anti-poverty policies

Children's own accounts of what it is like to be poor can increase our understanding of the impact on families of living on a low income. Here, Tess Ridge argues that for anti-poverty strategies to be successful, we need to allow children's own voices to be heard.

'You can't do as much, and I don't like my clothes and that, so I don't really get to do much or do stuff like my friends are doing . . . I am worried about what people think of me, like they think I am sad or something.'

Nicole, 13 years old

Nicole is a thirteen-year-old girl living on a housing estate in an inner city area of Bristol. She is one of a group of forty children who were interviewed as part of a new forthcoming study of childhood poverty. The study set out to develop an understanding of poverty in childhood that was drawn from the perspectives of poor children themselves, and provides an account of their lives that is grounded in their own realities and meanings. Nicole's quote encapsulates many of the issues and concerns that children and young people raised during the course of the study. The perception that because she was living in a family on a low income she was at risk of being excluded from the everyday social engagements and interactions that constitute part of the social experience of being a child. These anxieties about difference and stigma are apparent in her fear of being left out, and of being seen to be different from her peers.

Accounts from poor children give us a valuable insight into the lived experience of poverty in childhood, and contribute to our growing awareness of the importance of gaining a meaningful understanding of how the experience of poverty impacts on people's lives. This is particularly significant when thinking about childhood poverty and the impact of child poverty on children's lives, both in the immediacy of childhood and in later adult life. The new policy drive towards ending childhood poverty requires a greater engagement and involvement with low-income children and young people if our understandings of what poverty in childhood signifies for children themselves are to be fully realised and incorporated into policy and practice.

Childhood poverty

There has been an increasingly sophisticated programme of measurement and assessment of children in poverty, and we now have a good understanding about which children are in poverty, and the impact of factors such as worklessness, family structure, ill health, disability and ethnicity on the likelihood of children experiencing a spell of poverty in childhood. This is supported by considerable evidence about the potentially severe outcomes of childhood poverty, including poor health, low self-esteem, poor cognitive development and low educational achievement. However,

there is far less evidence and a much poorer understanding of the processes and factors that may underpin these data, and the social and emotional impact that either a transitory or a chronic spell of poverty in childhood can have on the life of the child. These effects need to be seen both in the short term (outcomes in childhood itself) and in the long term (outcomes in adulthood). We need to know how children experience poverty in the immediacy of childhood among their peers in their most formative social years, as well as having a concern for the outcomes in adulthood.

The relational impact of poverty on children's lives is a sorely neglected area. What evidence we do have comes in the main from studies that have involved adults' perceptions of children's needs. These show that children are particularly vulnerable to exclusion from items and activities perceived as socially necessary. Studies such as the *Small Fortunes Survey* and *Poverty and Social Exclusion in Britain* establish through research with adults a list of items and activities that are considered basic necessities for children in Britain today. Evidence from *Poverty and Social Exclusion in Britain*, using an index of socially perceived necessities, reveals the impact of poverty for children across a broad range of areas. This shows that one-third of British children go without at least one item or activity deemed as necessary by the majority of the population, and nearly one-fifth (18 per cent) go without two or more items or activities. The survey provides a particularly valuable insight into participation in social activities for children. However, valuable as these are, they all entail adult perceptions of children's needs; there has been little engagement with poor children themselves about things which they would consider essential for their material and social well-being.

Children on a low income 'begin to experience the reality of their differentness at an early age'

The few studies that have involved low-income children and young people in poverty research reveal the considerable pressures that they experience in all areas of their lives. *Family Fortunes* explores the economic pressures on parents and children in the UK, to provide a insight into the lives and experiences of children and their families. This was a seminal work in the field of understanding families' management of money and the pressures experienced in households with reduced incomes. It reveals the social pressures that children in general experience from their peers, and how children on a low income 'begin to experience the reality of their "differentness" at an early age'. These issues are further highlighted by two child-centred studies by the Children's Society. Same Scenery, *Different Lifestyle* highlighted the experiences of low-income children living in rural areas and found that they had a qualitatively different experience of rural life compared with their more affluent peers. *Worth More Than This* describes the impact of poverty on young people's physical and psychological health, their social lives and relationships and their education and aspirations. It is clear from these studies that engaging directly with low-income children and young people about their lives and experiences provides a valuable opportunity to gain a truer understanding of the social and material pressure that low-income children and young people face in their lives

The Government has shown a willingness to engage with children

Why talk to children?

For children, the impact of poverty is likely to spread across all areas of their lives, affecting their mental and physical health, their social relationships and their perceptions of the opportunities and choices open to them. Without an honest engagement with poor children that is open to understanding and acknowledging their different perceptions and meanings, we run the risk of over-looking or obscuring the very real and subjective experience of what it is like to be poor as a child. It is only recently that either researchers or policy-makers have sought the views and experiences of children and young people. However, there is now a growing interest within government and within research to understand how children are represented within the policy process and how they are engaged within policy and practice. There is also recognition that children and young people are not merely adults-in-waiting, but social actors in their own right, with their own issues and concerns. The Government has shown a willingness to engage with children and this is evident in a variety of consultation exercises with children and young people, especially 'looked after' children. Plus the involvement of children in the development of the new Children and Young People's Unit and the administration of the new Children's Fund. However, these are early days in the process of consultation and participation, and if the exercise is to prove fruitful, children from all walks of life need to be included in the process.

In general, people in poverty are rarely asked to contribute to an understanding or definition of what poverty means for them as a lived experience. This is especially so for children, whose lives and experiences, whilst currently very much in the policy spotlight, have in general tended to be doubly obscured, both as children and as part of the 'unheard' constituency of the poor. As such their views and concerns have remained largely absent from both public policy and poverty research. Yet, without a more informed understanding of childhood poverty and its impact on children, policies designed to alleviate child poverty and improve the lives of poor children run the risk of failing.

Dr Tess Ridge works in the Department of Social and Policy Sciences at the University of Bath

■ The above information is an extract from *Poverty* 111, Winter 2002, the magazine produced by the Child Poverty Action Group. For the full article and footnotes visit their web site at www.cpag.org.uk/info/Poverty_articles/Poverty111/children.htm

Still Missing Out

'Gaps remain in Government's fight against child poverty,' says Barnardo's

Disabled children are 'Still Missing Out' in the fight to eradicate child poverty, says the UK's largest children's charity, Barnardo's.

Barnardo's remains very concerned at the plight of disabled children, despite acknowledging the Prime Minister's speech this morning, renewing the Government's commitment to eradicate child poverty by 2020.

'The Government must focus on the plight of disabled children and their families', says Neera Sharma, Barnardo's Principal Policy Officer. Barnardo's report 'Still Missing Out' shows that many of these children are still missing out on the basic necessities of an ordinary life.

'Still Missing Out' says that if the Government is to end child poverty within a generation, it will need to tackle the causes of poverty and social exclusion by providing suitable childcare for disabled children, providing accessible housing and providing the support needed by those who are working or for parents who wish to find work.

Neera Sharma adds: 'The Government has pledged to end child poverty within a generation. However, there is little evidence from our report to show that their initiatives to date are significantly improving the lives of the UK's 360,000 disabled children.'

■ The above information is from Barnardo's web site: www.barnardos.org.uk

North-south gap likely to widen, warn researchers

By Peter Hetherington, Regional Affairs Editor

Divisions between London and the big cities of the north and the Midlands are continuing to widen because the government has set its face against any strategy to spread the wealth of the booming south to provincial England, according to new research.

Outlining a continuing regional polarisation into a 'two nation country', it questions why the north-south economic gap continued to widen during the growing prosperity of the past five years, when poorer cities should have caught up with the capital rather than falling further behind.

The research, by a leading academic who advises the government, complements another study by senior planners and economists for the country's 30 big urban authorities, which says northern conurbations have been losing ground to London, the south-east and East Anglia since 1993, and show no sign of catching up.

The study warns that growing north-south disparities in England contrast markedly with the experience of capital and provincial cities in mainland Europe.

'This widening gap in relative economic fortunes occurred during a national economic upswing when regional convergence (with London and the south) would have been expected, as indeed happened across the European Union as a whole,' it says.

'All the social and economic indicators reinforce the view that there is a wide, and growing gulf between the north-east, north-west, Yorkshire and Humberside and the west Midlands on the one hand, and London, the south-east and east on the other, and that large cities are especially vulnerable.'

Produced by Manchester University's Centre for Urban Policy Studies, the Greater London Group at the London School of Economics, and Leeds University's department of geography, the recently completed study will strengthen arguments of Labour backbenchers in the party's heartlands who believe the government is doing little to narrow a north-south divide.

> **'All the social and economic indicators reinforce the view that there is a wide, and growing gulf'**

It comes as the Core Cities Group, representing Birmingham, Bristol, Nottingham, Sheffield, Liverpool, Manchester, Leeds and Newcastle upon Tyne, meets for its annual conference in Manchester where the local government and regions minister, Stephen Byers, is to give an address today.

While he has acknowledged an 'unacceptable' north-south divide, critics say the government has offered few solutions.

This week Mr Byers said that he was pitching for several billion pounds from the Treasury in the forthcoming three-year comprehensive spending review, in order to rescue blighted northern neighbourhoods – close to seemingly booming city centres such as Manchester and Newcastle – where property markets are collapsing due to low demand for houses, a sure sign of a continuing economic downturn in big cities.

In a separate report published yesterday, Brian Robson, head of Manchester University's urban policy centre, said that London was now creating twice as many jobs as the core cities.

He has calculated that while employment growth in London rose by 17.4% in the late 90s alone, the core cities showed a rise of under 10%, and a much lower rise of 5.4% if their surrounding conurbations are thrown into the equation.

He warned: 'There is nothing . . . to gainsay the view that there is a continuing polarisation of England with a booming south and a lagging north and west.'

Studies undertaken by Ivan Turok, professor of urban economic development at Glasgow University, have already shown that Britain's 20 leading cities have lost over 500,000 jobs since 1981, while the rest of the country gained at least 1.7m.

NORTH

THE GREAT GULF

SOUTH

Richest 10% spend seven times more than poorest

By John Carvel, Social Affairs Editor

The gap between rich and poor was demonstrated yesterday by official figures showing that the 10% of households in the top income bracket spent nearly seven times as much as the 10% with the lowest incomes.

In an average week the richest 10th spent £849, including £187.50 on leisure items such as cinema, theatre, television, holidays, gambling and gardening. The poorest 10th spent £126.70, including £20.20 on leisure.

This latest slant on inequality in the UK came in the family expenditure survey for 2000-01 published yesterday by the office for national statistics.

It showed average household spending (excluding taxes, savings and purchase of capital goods) was £390 a week. The biggest outlay was on leisure, with households averaging just over £70 a week on spare-time activities, compared with £64 on housing, £62 on food and non-alcoholic drink and £55 on motoring.

Spending on leisure goods and services increased by 10% last year, accounting for 18% of household spending. Higher mortgage costs caused spending on housing to

Who has what?

- Of the poorest households 75% have a washing machine but only 4% a dishwasher, against 68% of highest income households
- Average weekly spending on mobile phones rose by 500% from 1995 to 1999 to £2, and to £2.10 in 2000/01, with fixed lines at £5.80
- Spending on clothing and footwear averaged £22 a week in 2000/01
- Spending on milk fell by 25% to £2.10 between 1995 and 2000/01

overtake food and drink as the second biggest item in the family budget.

The richest 10th of the population spent 42% more than the second richest 10th. Average weekly outgoings for the richest were: £145.80 on leisure services and £41.70 on leisure goods, £141.10 on housing, £118.30 on motoring, £111.40 on food and non-alcoholic drinks,

£70.60 on household goods, £54.80 on household services, £45.80 on clothing and footwear, £33.80 on alcohol, £32.70 on personal goods and services, £28.20 on fares, £16.60 on fuel and power, £6.50 on tobacco and £1.60 on sundries.

Weekly outgoings for the poorest 10th were: £25.80 on food and non-alcoholic drinks, £21 on housing, £14.10 on leisure services and £6.10 on leisure goods, £11.20 on household goods, £8.60 on fuel and power, £8.60 on motoring, £8.50 on household services, £6.70 on clothing and footwear, £5 on personal goods and services, £4.20 on alcohol, £3.90 on tobacco, £2.70 on fares and 20p on sundries.

The ONS said the spending gap was slightly higher than 12 months before when the richest 10th averaged £782 a week and the poorest £120. But proportionately the gap was greater 10 years ago when the richest spent £513 and the poorest £69. The figures are not adjusted for inflation.

The survey showed average household spending in rural areas was higher than in all other parts of the country except London. In spite of the low incomes of many rural workers, average weekly spending was £420 a week, compared with £460 in the London built-up areas and £320 in small towns.

Spending was highest in London, the south and eastern region, and lowest in north-east England. Londoners spent 19% of their income on housing, 3% above the national average, while in Northern Ireland housing accounted for 10%.

Those living in the north-east spent the most on alcohol, averaging £16.50 a week, compared with a national average of £14.80.

The survey was based on information from 6,500 people through the UK who kept a two-week diary of outgoings.

Poverty and young motherhood

A new report by the YWCA, to be presented to the UN, highlights the link between poverty and early motherhood

The YWCA is calling on the Government to step up its commitment to eradicate poverty and social exclusion of young parents, after a new study highlighted the strong links between poverty and teenage motherhood.

The report, *Poverty: The Price of Young Motherhood in Britain*, was presented to a United Nations Commission in New York on 7 March 2002. The author of the report, the YWCA's Director of Policy and Campaigns, Mandana Hendessi, is urging people to stop demonising teenage mothers and puts forward a seven-point action plan to improve the plight of young parents in the UK, which still has the highest levels of teenage pregnancy and child poverty in western Europe.

The report includes a review of recent research and two separate studies carried out by the YWCA, comprising interviews with a total of 136 mothers in England and 26 agencies working with them. The interviews support recent research showing that poverty, low educational attainment and poor self-esteem combine to form a vicious circle for young women in the most deprived areas of the UK, where the highest rates of early motherhood occur. Above all, the social stigmatisation of teenage parenthood and lone motherhood, in particular, has led to teenage mothers shying away from essential services.

There are also worrying findings in the report about young women from Bangladeshi and Pakistani communities, showing that restrictive family and cultural values often lead to Asian women having limited access to health and social services.

Whilst Ms Hendessi's report welcomes existing government initiatives to tackle poverty and social exclusion in the UK, it calls

for wider measures to help young women. She said: 'Britain is the fourth richest industrial nation and yet we still have the highest rate of teenage pregnancy and child poverty in western Europe. We must act now to eradicate poverty and social exclusion. Crucially, it is time to stop demonising young mums.

'Evidence has shown time and again that young women do not get pregnant to get housing and welfare benefits; most of them, in fact, don't know about welfare entitlements before they get pregnant.

As part of its action plan, the YWCA is calling on the Government to:

- Tackle the poverty experienced by young adults by increasing the minimum wage for those aged 21 and under to the adult rate
- Establish courses for all health and social care professionals on the issues and needs of young parents
- Fund childcare provision at further education and higher education colleges to encourage enrolment by young mothers
- Challenge the social stigma surrounding teenage pregnancy and motherhood by publicising existing research which has resolutely dispelled the myths about teenage motherhood

---

'The public hysteria about teenage mothers is unjustified and contributes to negative attitudes sometimes held by health and social care professionals, ironically the very people whose job it is to help teenage mothers. Such attitudes deter young women from accessing services at times when they are especially in need of assistance.'

Oxfam UK, who part-funded the research, welcomed the YWCA's report and recommendations. Oxfam Gender Advisor, Sue Smith, said:

'Teenage mothers are amongst the poorest and most vulnerable people in the UK. This research is a timely investigation of how early motherhood is a poverty trap for young women. It provides important insights into the lives of the young women interviewed and offers solutions that will help Oxfam and the YWCA in their anti-poverty work in Great Britain.'

YWCA projects in some of the most deprived areas of England and Wales are already helping young women break the cycle of poverty and lack of opportunity. The charity provides a wide range of services for disadvantaged young women, many of whom are already mothers in their teens. The YWCA has led the way in providing on-site childcare, so that young mothers excluded from school or who have failed to gain qualifications can attend training and get back into education or into work.

- *Poverty: The Price of Young Motherhood in Britain* by Mandana Hendessi and Frahana Rashid is published by the YWCA and supported by Oxfam UK. ISBN: 0-901862-11-8. Price £8.

- The above information is from the YWCA of Great Britain. Visit their web site at www.ywca-gb.org.uk

Plight of pensioners

Plight of pensioners in deprived areas shocking, says Help the Aged; calls on Government to end pensioner poverty

The lives of many older people living in deprived areas of England's cities are blighted by poverty, crime and isolation, according to a new study. The study, published by Help the Aged, draws on research supported by the Economic and Social Research Council through its Growing Older Programme.

Mervyn Kohler, Head of Public Affairs at Help the Aged, said: 'The shocking poverty and low quality of life experienced by so many older people in the most deprived areas of our country is a disgrace. The Government must re-examine its priorities and pledge to end pensioner poverty, as it has pledged to end poverty for children.'

The Charity accuses the Government's Social Exclusion Unit of 'ignoring older people' when addressing social exclusion and calls for a specific commitment from the unit to take account of the needs of older people.

The research, carried out by the Centre for Social Gerontology at Keele University in the most deprived electoral wards in Liverpool, Manchester and Newham in East London, reveals that two-thirds of older people in these areas have to cope with medium or high levels of deprivation and that 45 per cent are living in poverty.

Fear of crime is endemic among older people in deprived areas, with much justification. Forty per cent of older people in these areas have been the victim of one or more type of crime in the recent past. This flies in the face of the accepted wisdom that older people are less likely to be the victims of crime.

The report points out that the Government's attempt to tackle poverty in a 'targeted' way, by using the Minimum Income Guarantee, 'often appears to break down before reaching those experiencing greatest need'.

- More than one in ten older people find it 'difficult' or 'very difficult' to manage on their current incomes.
- Fifteen per cent of older people living in poverty had, on occasion, gone without buying food.
- Older people from minority ethnic backgrounds are worse off; eight out of ten older Somalis and seven out of ten older Pakistanis are living in poverty.

Many older people are living in a hostile environment that is degraded and neglected. Often, they are deprived of amenities that most of us take for granted, such as a local Post Office, health and social care, welfare services, or safe and reliable transport. Meanwhile, despite their commitment to their neighbourhoods, they find that town planners and central government make no effort to listen to their problems and learn from their experiences.

The work of the Government's Social Exclusion Unit since 1997 has tended to concentrate on young families and children in poverty and unemployed people of working age, often overlooking the circumstances of older people, who have the least chance of improving their lives. It is time to redress the balance. Help the Aged believes that:

- The Government must match their pledge to wipe out child poverty by 2020 with a pledge to rid the country of pensioner poverty by the same year.
- The Social Exclusion Unit itself excludes older people in its work, and calls on the Unit to make specific commitments to a timetable for recognising the needs of senior citizens in future projects.
- Central and local government must move older people to centre stage in the planning and regeneration process, and must put in place practical guidance and help to improve everyday life for some of the UK's most deprived citizens.

Dr Thomas Scharf, Senior Lecturer in Social Gerontology at the University of Keele, and an author of the report, said: 'It is unacceptable that so many older people in our cities are living in poverty and deprivation, are experiencing crime, and are cut off from other people. This research demonstrates the many difficulties faced by older people in deprived areas, raising important questions for society as a whole. In particular, there is a need to develop an idea of what an 'acceptable old age' might look like. Improving the quality of daily life for older people in deprived areas should become a goal for government on a local and national level.'

- The above information is from Help the Aged's web site which can be found at www.helptheaged.org.uk

© Help the Aged

Ensuring that women live free from poverty

Financial security

Key facts

- Over 45% of women have a gross individual income of less than £100 a week, compared to just over 20% of men.
- There is a 20% hourly pay gap between women and men working full time.

Equal pay

In all sectors and at all levels women earn less than men. There is a 20% hourly pay gap between women and men working full time. The weekly earnings gap is even wider than the pay gap – women working full time earn 73.8% of full time men's weekly wage.

Women working part time earn even less per hour. Women working part time earn 60% of the hourly wage of men working full time. Over a lifetime it is estimated that the gender pay gap can cost a mid-skilled woman without children just under £250,000.

If men and women had equal pay, it would make a significant contribution to ending child poverty, help women achieve their full potential and end the cycle of lifetime inequality that results in women's poverty in old age.

Low pay

4.7 million women earn less than £5 an hour – 43% of all women employees. Half of all women working full time and 80% of those working part time earn below the Council of Europe's decency threshold of £6.31 an hour.

Low pay is an issue not only for those women on low wages, but also for those who depend on them such as their children.

Women on low pay are unable to build up savings. If they earn too little to make National Insurance contributions they are unable to claim contributory benefits such as the basic state pension or statutory sick pay.

Women's low pay over a lifetime makes them vulnerable to poverty in old age.

Pensions

More than twice as many older women as men are reliant on income support.

Nearly two-fifths of female pensioners have incomes of under £100 a week.

A combination of low pay and time out of the workplace for caring responsibilities means that many women live in poverty in old age. Women have suffered from a welfare system that was developed around men's patterns of lifetime earnings. The system assumed that women would be able to rely on their husband's pension to support them in old age. However, the legacy of policies like these is that older women living alone are among the poorest pensioners.

The tax and benefit system

Women are more likely than men to be dependent on means-tested benefits and less likely to be higher-rate taxpayers.

The tax and benefit system contains a number of assumptions that have altered little since the 1940s. For example the calculation of pension entitlement is based on a working life that consists of continuous employment from 16 to 65. Family based assessment and payment of benefits to the 'head of the household' reflect an assumption of dependency between husbands and wives.

Caring responsibilities

Women still take the main responsibility for caring for children and for sick, elderly or disabled family members. These caring responsibilities mean that women are more likely to work part time and to have time out of paid work. This results in a lower lifetime income and all too often poverty in old age.

Income within households

There is a strong belief that families share income and decisions about how to spend money. However, a growing body of evidence suggests that, for many, the egalitarian family is a myth.

Most couples share financial decision making. However, a fifth of women say their husband/partner has the final say.

24% of women with personal incomes of less than £400 a month said their husband or partner made big financial decisions compared with 12% of women with an income of between £1200 and £1600.

The Women's Budget Group

The Women's Budget Group (WBG) is an independent organisation bringing together academics and people from non-governmental organisations and trade unions to promote gender equality through appropriate economic policy.

If you would like more information about the work of the WBG, or to join the group and contribute to the work, please look on our website: www.wbg.org.uk

- The above information is from the Fawcett Society's web site: www.fawcettsociety.org.uk

Benefit will help fight child poverty

By Jill Papworth

The new child tax credit, payable to nearly six million families from April 2003 and the government's main weapon in its fight to abolish child poverty, received a warm welcome last night.

The credit, which will combine all income-related support for children into a single payment made direct to the main carer, usually the mother, will be payable to all families with incomes of up to £58,000 (£66,000 in the first year of a child's life) – a much higher than expected threshold.

It will be paid at a maximum weekly rate of £27.75 per child on top of universal child benefit, which goes to all parents regardless of their income. Where possible, it will be paid directly into the carer's bank account.

The 25% of families with an annual income of less than £13,000 will get the maximum child tax credit (CTC). Combined with child benefit, this will give them £54.25 a week for the first child and £38.50 for each subsequent child. So, for example, the poorest families with two children will get £92.75.

The National Council for One Parent Families calculates that the poorest lone parents with two children will be £11 a week better off under CTC than on current income support levels.

For families on incomes of more than £13,000, the level of CTC payment will taper away gradually until disappearing completely for those on £58,000 or more, who will receive only child benefit at £16.05 per week for the first child and £10.75 for subsequent children.

For households with two children, for example, this means £37.25 a week for the 50% of families who are on incomes of between £13,000 and £50,000, while those on £58,000 or more will get £26.80 a week.

CTC brings together into one payment all means-tested, income-related support for children. It will integrate and replace the child elements of the working families' tax credit, the disabled person's tax credit and income support or jobseeker's allowance, as well as the existing children's tax credit introduced in April 2001.

There will be no work conditions attached to the CTC. The amount paid will be assessed purely on the basis of the family income for the previous tax year. Family can mean an individual, or a married or cohabiting couple.

This means CTC will be extended to some groups who are currently excluded from all but child benefit, such as students.

Kate Green, director of NCOPF, says: 'We welcome this as a forward-looking Budget. Child tax credit at this level will make a real difference

to the poorest families and the commitment to increase CTC levels at least in line with earnings each year will help ensure that the poorest children do not fall further behind.

> *The amount paid will be assessed purely on the basis of the family income for the previous tax year. Family can mean an individual, or a married or co-habiting couple*

'But further significant increases in CTC will be needed if the government is to meet its pledge of eradicating child poverty by the year 2020.'

Ms Green also applauded the chancellor's decision to extend help with childcare costs to low-income families, especially parents working shifts or with disabled children, who need childcare provided in their own home.

From April 2003 they will be able to claim tax credits if they use a home childcarer, a domiciliary care worker or a nurse employed through a registered care agency.

Martin Barnes, director of the Child Poverty Action Group, also welcomed the Budget as 'brave, positive and showing a clear commitment to tackling child poverty'.

Also from April 2003, flat-rate statutory maternity pay, which is paid after the first six weeks' leave, will go up from £75 to £100 a week. Maternity allowance, paid to self-employed women and others not eligible for the statutory pay, will also go up to the same rate.

Working fathers, for the first time, will get the right to two weeks' paternity leave at the same £100 rate.

It's all for the sake of the children

Ministers have pledged to abolish child poverty within two decades – but all the signs are that it will be a tough challenge. Gideon Burrows reports

Mrs K was a 33-year-old single mother with five children. The family shared a one-bedroom maisonette, where Mum bunked with the two boys and the girls had to sleep in the loft. Every night they crawled through a hole in the wall, over exposed pipes and wires, to get to bed.

It was only when a local newspaper reported the scandal that the family was found a four-bedroom home. But after the move, they had no money for clothes, and no spare cash to buy carpets or furniture to make their new home habitable.

This is a real example of child poverty, one of the cases dealt with recently by workers with the Family Welfare Association. There are many more.

Tony Blair came to power in 1997 with the ambitious promise of eradicating child poverty in the UK 'within a generation'. Since then, the targets have been clarified: to cut child poverty by one-quarter by 2005, by one-half five years later, and completely by 2020.

Over four million children – approximately one in three – are still poor

Both the statistics and the stories of people like Mrs K reveal that there is much work to do.

In December a survey by the Joseph Rowntree Foundation and the New Policy Institute, *Monitoring poverty and social exclusion 2001*, revealed the slow pace of progress. The number of children living below the poverty line fell by only 300,000 between the 1997 election and the end of the century. Over four million children – approximately one in three – are still poor.

Labour claimed during the last election to have lifted 1.2 million children out of poverty, but then clarified that the figure included children who would have become poor had the party not taken control in 1997.

There is a continuing debate about what 'poverty' means, and how it is measured. The Treasury defines it as including households earning less than 60% of the median UK income, after paying for housing. But that definition has important weaknesses.

'While it tells us about the distribution of incomes, it tells us nothing about the level of need represented,' says the Child Poverty Action Group, which last month published a compendium of statistics: *Poverty: the facts*.

Chancellor Gordon Brown has a two-pronged strategy to deal with child poverty. It concentrates on providing more money directly, but also on improving life opportunities.

The measures to improve cash income include the minimum wage, increased child benefit, the children's tax credit and the working families' tax credit. The government claims personal tax and benefit changes already mean that families with children are £1,000 a year richer.

But the chancellor's crowning glory is likely to be the integrated child tax credit, to be introduced in April 2003. The package will bring together the child-related portions of other benefits like income and housing support, and deliver it in a simpler, integrated, and more generous form after means testing. The credit is intended to free up more money for parents to bring their families above the poverty line, as well as providing them with the means to go into work.

But a new system may do little to help without more generous cash backing. The Institute of Fiscal Studies has estimated the April budget will need to allocate £5bn specifically for the credit if the government is to hit its child poverty target.

Children from ethnic minorities, asylum seekers and children in very large families are likely to remain chronically poor

'The level will determine whether child poverty will be eradicated or not,' says Neera Sharma, policy officer on child poverty at Barnardo's.

If the government concentrates its efforts on improving cash income, it will only reach 1.5 million of the least poor children below the poverty line, Barnardo's claims. Over two million more will remain consistently and chronically poor because of the lack of work opportunities and child care.

'The current measures will be successful to a limit, but the government will have to do more to access those hardest to reach. There need to be specific targets and strategies to take these poorest children out of poverty,' says Ms Sharma.

Children from ethnic minorities, asylum seekers and children in very large families are likely to remain chronically poor. The Family Welfare Association hears many such cases.

Mrs N, an asylum seeker from Nigeria, had two children due to enter secondary school. She is registered disabled, but as an asylum seeker is not entitled to disabled living allowance, nor can she work. Her 12-year-old son, the main carer for the family, recently received a letter saying he would not be admitted to secondary school without a £107 uniform, money the family cannot spare.

Other problems with a strategy that concentrates on increasing cash income are that it provides only a temporary income top-up, in the hope that will lead to better life chances for children in the longer term; and it depends on a sound national economy, where jobs exist and government coffers can spare generous tax benefits for the poor.

It may be the second half of the government strategy that will do most in the long term.

By 2004, the Sure Start programme aims to have launched more than 500 projects nationwide to improve 'the health and well-being of families and children before and from birth'. The new Connexions youth service provides integrated advice, guidance and personal development opportunities for teenagers, 'to help them make a smooth transition to adulthood and working life'. Both aim to improve opportunities for the poorest children and families, without providing cash handouts.

These programmes are relatively new, and their effectiveness will only begin to emerge with the publication of government poverty figures in July.

Campaigners point to other issues which the government must tackle before it can be confident of achieving its child poverty targets.

'The government has been twiddling its thumbs on the Social Fund since it was elected,' says Martin Barnes, director of the Child Poverty Action Group. 'The fund needs a radical overhaul.'

The Social Fund is supposed to provide one-off payments to poor households for essential purchases like a fridge or cooker, but because the cash is strictly limited, families can be turned down even when they desperately need help. The fund also provides loans to families, which, according to a recent survey by Barnardo's, can push families who borrow even deeper into poverty.

The Family Welfare Association heard the story of a single mother aged 26, with young children, who had to move to escape domestic violence. She received £93.85 a week

Action so far: the government's record

- Child benefit rose by 26% in real terms since 1997, to £15.50 per week for the oldest child.
- Working families' tax credit introduced, a means-tested benefit to help parents in work. Added an average £79.58 to the weekly income of 1.26 million low-paid families.
- National minimum wage, currently worth £4.10 per hour for adults in work.
- Sure Start maternity grant increased from £200 to £300 in September 2000.
- Introduction in April 2000 of a children's tax credit at £10 a week for all parents earning under £32,000 a year.
- Children and Young People's Unit was launched in 2000 to co-ordinate children's strategies across government, and to improve services for children.
- Children's Fund established to fund local partnerships improving services for children, and for specific projects to generate opportunities for socially excluded children.
- New deal for lone parents now available to all lone parents who are jobless or working less than 16 hours a week.
- Sure Start launched to strengthen families and local communities with support services for very young children in deprived areas. Planned annual expenditure is almost £500m by 2004.
- The Connexions service launched to provide teenagers in England with help and support, particularly helping those at risk of social exclusion. By the end of 2002/03 the government will invest £420m.

income support and her outgoings totalled £93.49. The family desperately needed a bed, bedding for the eldest son, a cot and bedding for the baby, and carpets for some rooms in the house. Ms D was refused a Social Fund loan because she was already repaying previous loans at the maximum she could afford.

The Commons select committee on work and pensions has said the fund is in danger of undermining the government's anti-poverty strategy, yet it remains in place.

Plans in the pipeline

- Sure Start maternity grant will increase to £500 from April 2002.
- Integrated child tax credit to be introduced from April 2003, bringing together child-related help currently contained in income support, jobseeker's allowance, and other benefits. Levels and thresholds will be announced in April.
- Working/employment tax credit to be introduced from April 2003 for all poor working people, with or without children. Levels and thresholds also to be announced in April.

The lack of affordable and reliable childcare also contributes to poverty because it prevents poor parents from working. 'If [the government] is to meet the challenge of ending child poverty, then early years childcare and education services must be integrated on a universal basis,' the Daycare Trust says.

Poverty campaigners are waiting anxiously for the summer, when the chancellor sets spending levels for the next three years for his anti-poverty programmes in the comprehensive spending review.

To pull the maximum number of children out of poverty, there needs to be generous support – at a time when pressure to bankroll mainstream public services like health and education is greater than ever.

- *Monitoring poverty and social exclusion 2001*: www.jrf.org.uk/ knowledge/findings/socialpolicy/ pdf/D31.pdf
- *Poverty: the facts*: www.cpag.org.uk
- Institute for Fiscal Studies: www.ifs.org.uk

- The above information is an extract from the magazine *New Start*: www.newstartmag.co.uk

© *New Start*

'More needs to be done to tackle child poverty'

By David Batty

The government has admitted that its efforts to reduce poverty have yet to improve the lives of most disadvantaged children.

The admission came in the latest annual poverty survey by the Department of Work and Pensions, which noted there was 'undeniably' more to do in tackling deprivation.

The prime minister, Tony Blair, said for the first time in a speech today that if Labour was to meet its pledge to end child poverty within a generation it would require the redistribution of wealth from the haves to the have-nots.

In the forward to the new report the work and pensions secretary, Andrew Smith, pledged the government would redouble its efforts to combat the poverty that 'blights people's lives and denies opportunity to their children'.

He said 'good progress' was being made in tackling the root causes of poverty but admitted there was 'still a lot of work to do'.

Indicators of social exclusion showed that significant progress had been made in many areas since 1996.

But the report, *Opportunity For All*, showed that the suicide rate has risen and the number of pupils excluded from school is also increasing.

There was also no significant improvement in the number of people suffering persistently low incomes in Britain, adult smoking rates, use of class A drugs, such as heroin, and the number of English 16- to 18-year-olds in education.

The report emphasised the important role of public services in improving the well-being of those on low incomes, and noted that they would have to significantly improve if government targets were to be met.

'In public services, arguably more than any other area, we recognise how much more we have to do. We do not underestimate the enormity of the challenge,' it said.

The work and pensions secretary said new tax credits will be introduced to cut child poverty while child support arrangements will be reviewed, to ensure that more benefit from maintenance.

The report added that the expansion of Sure Start programmes to help disadvantaged families would help ensure that the needs of more vulnerable children were met and their problems were identified earlier.

It pledged that by 2006 an extra 300,000 children will have access to health, education and other services.

Notable achievements highlighted in the report include the record number of people in work, which has risen by more than 1.5m since 1997 to 27.7m.

Poverty 'blights people's lives and denies opportunity to their children'

Half a million fewer children were living in relatively low income households last year compared with 1996-97, and the average pensioner would soon be £1,150 a year better off than in 1997.

The report reiterated the government's commitment to eradicating child poverty in a generation, achieving full employment, providing security for those unable to work and ensuring that older people can live secure lives.

'Our goal is to improve all of these areas of people's lives and tackle the root causes of poverty,' it stated.

The next steps would include more childcare provision, job opportunities for lone parents and the disabled, and extending the 'rights and responsibilities' approach to employment.

New-style job centres will be opened across the country and by 2006 an extra two million people will have a personal interview from a job adviser, he added.

More support would be given to pensioners on low or modest incomes over the next few years and there will be proposals later this year to reform private pensions to encourage more saving for retirement.

However, Martin Barnes, the director of the Child Poverty Action Group, expressed concern that the government was 'picking and mixing' its definitions of poverty.

The government announced plans to redefine poverty in April, after it failed to meet its target of taking 1.2 million children out of poverty.

Mr Barnes said that rushing to adopt new measurements would amount to a 'blatant and transparent moving of the goalposts'.

He added that there were still significant gaps in services for vulnerable children and families.

There was need for urgent reform of housing benefit and the social fund, which is meant to provide low income households with financial help for essential items or in emergencies.

Mr Barnes said: 'The fund is only £100m for the whole of England and there is clear evidence that families are being denied help because it is cash-limited.'

Beating child poverty

UK public wants more action from world leaders to beat child poverty

MORI research shows clearly that the UK public believes that child poverty can be beaten – and they want world leaders to do more. 90% would be willing to help the fight against child poverty themselves if asked by a charity and would be prepared to take an active part in lobbying governments; sign a petition; display a poster or sticker; support fair trade or give their own time or money to support a campaign.

The poll comes at a time when the debate on child poverty is high on the international agenda. It reveals an overwhelming majority of the population views global child poverty as a serious political issue – and that they believe that more should be done to combat it.

More than half of UK adults interviewed said they would like to see Tony Blair or the UK Government taking more action to combat child poverty in the UK. In contrast tackling child poverty in developing countries is thought to be the responsibility of the UN, World Bank and the IMF – all came under fire for not doing enough.

The research shows that the public is largely optimistic about the likelihood of eliminating child poverty, especially in the UK. However, when asked about the ability of governments to meet targets on child poverty, people's optimism plummets. The MORI poll shows that less than half the UK public has faith in government or official targets to combat this problem.

The key findings of the poll show:
- 98% identified child poverty as a serious political issue in developing countries; 60% say the same is true for the UK
- 64% of people agreed that child poverty in the UK can be ended, and 38% agreed that this was the case globally
- This falls to 46% when presented with the UK government targets to reduce child poverty in the

UK by half within ten years – and to eliminate it within 20 years – and 24% when presented with the UN's world-wide 'Millennium Target' to halve the global percentage of people living in extreme poverty by 2015

More than half of UK adults interviewed said they would like to see Tony Blair or the UK Government taking more action to combat child poverty in the UK

- 56% would like to see Tony Blair and the UK Government taking more action to combat child poverty
- 56% of people identified the UN

as having lead responsibility for eradicating child poverty globally followed by the World Bank/IMF (41%)
- 90% of UK adults would be prepared to do something to help end child poverty, if asked by a charity
- 26% of UK adults would be prepared to do four or more things to help combat child poverty, if asked by a charity

Note:
MORI interviewed a representative quota sample of 2,095 adults aged 15+ in 201 sampling points throughout the UK, between 21 and 26 March 2002. All interviews were conducted face-to-face and in homes. All data are weighted to the known national population profile.

- The above information is from MORI's web site which can be found at www.mori.com

© 2002 MORI

Child poverty in different families

The table below shows the poverty rate of children living in different family types in each Organisation for Economic Co-operation and Development (OECD) nation.

	Poverty rate of children in:	
	Lone-parent families	Other families
Turkey	29.2	19.6
Spain	31.6	11.8
Italy	22.2	20.4
Greece	24.9	11.8
Mexico	27.6	26.1
Poland	19.9	15.1
Luxembourg	30.4	2.9
Hungary	10.4	10.3
Netherlands	23.6	6.5
France	26.1	6.4
Ireland	46.4	14.2
Belgium	13.5	3.6
Czech Republic	30.9	3.6
Germany	51.2	6.2
Finland	7.1	3.9
Canada	51.6	10.4
Australia	35.6	8.8
Norway	13.1	2.2
Denmark	13.8	3.6
USA	55.4	15.8
UK	45.6	13.3
Sweden	6.7	1.5

Source: Child Poverty in Rich Nations, UNICEF

Poverty

Information from CAFOD

4.4 billion people live in developing countries. Of these:

- three-fifths lack basic sanitation
- almost one-third have no access to clean water
- a quarter do not have adequate housing
- a fifth have no access to modern health services
- a fifth of children do not attend to the end of primary school
- a fifth do not have adequate protein and energy from their food supplies

'Everyone has the right to a standard of living adequate for the health and well-being of him(her)self and his/her family, including food, clothing, housing and medical care and necessary social services . . . Everyone has the right to education.'

Universal Declaration of
Human Rights

Mind the gap

In 1997 the richest fifth of the world's population had 74 times the income of the poorest fifth.

The top three billionaires have assets greater than the combined GNP of all least developed countries and their 600 million people.

Human Development Report 1999

Things can only get better

Over 80 countries have lower incomes per person today than they did ten years ago.

Human Development Report 1999

Measuring poverty

According to internationally accepted standards anyone earning less than 60p a day (US $1) is living below the poverty line, i.e., does not earn enough to live on.

Percentage of people living below the poverty line

Europe and Central Asia	3.5%
Latin America and the Caribbean	23.5%

What is poverty?

'Not having the minimum income level to get the necessities of life.'
Concise Oxford Dictionary

'More than a lack of what is necessary for material well-being, poverty can also mean the denial of opportunities and choices most basic to human development – to lead a long, healthy, creative life; to have a decent standard of living.'
The State of Human Development 1998

Sub-Saharan Africa	38.5%
Middle East and North Africa	4.1%
South Asia	43.1%

There are three major ways of measuring a country's wealth:

- Gross National Product (GNP) is the annual total value of all goods produced and services provided in a country
- Gross Domestic Product (GDP) is the same, excluding deals with other countries
- Human Poverty Index (HPI) does not use money as the only factor. It includes education, length of life and living standards

(For more information see *Human Development Reports* since 1997)

Causes of third world poverty

Trade

Third world countries lose out through unfair trade agreements, lack of technology and investment, and rapidly changing prices for their goods.

Work and globalisation

Better communications and transport have led to a 'globalised' economy. Companies look for low-cost countries to invest in. This can mean that, though there are jobs, they are low-paid.

Debt

Third world countries have to pay interest on their debts. This means they cannot afford to spend enough on basic services like health and education; nor on things like transport or communications that might attract investment.

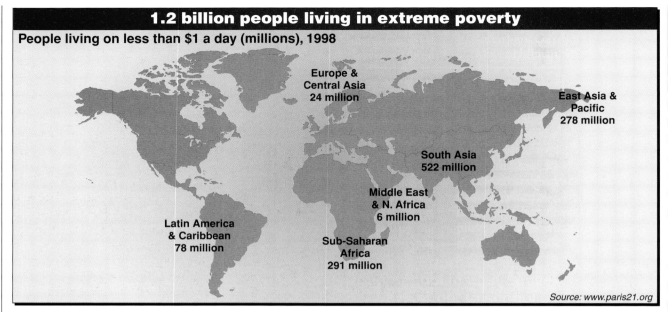

1.2 billion people living in extreme poverty

People living on less than $1 a day (millions), 1998

Europe &
Central Asia
24 million

East Asia &
Pacific
278 million

South Asia
522 million

Middle East
& N. Africa
6 million

Latin America
& Caribbean
78 million

Sub-Saharan
Africa
291 million

Source: www.paris21.org

Land

If you have land you can grow your own food. But many people in the third world have had their land taken over by large businesses, often to grow crops for export.

War or conflict

When a country is at war (including civil war) basic services like education are disrupted. People leave their homes as refugees. Crops are destroyed.

Health

Affordable or free health care is necessary for development. In poor countries the percentage of children who die under the age of five is much higher than in rich countries. HIV/AIDS is having a devastating effect on the third world.

'HIV is now the single greatest threat to future economic development in Africa. AIDS kills adults in the prime of their working and parenting lives, decimates the work force, fractures and impoverishes families, orphans millions . . .'

Callisto Madavo, vice-president of the World Bank, Africa region 1999.

Food and education

Affordable, secure food supplies are vital. Malnutrition causes severe health problems, and can also affect education. Without education it is difficult to escape from poverty. This becomes a vicious circle: people who live in poverty cannot afford to send their children to school.

Tackling poverty

2015 poverty targets

Members of the Organisation for Co-operation and Development (OECD) agreed these after the 1995 Copenhagen summit. They aim to reduce poverty in third world countries by at least one-half by 2015.

20/20 initiative

At the same summit some governments agreed that 20% of aid and 20% of the budget of the developing country receiving that aid would be spent on basic services.

Aid

Access to basic services for everyone would cost approximately US$40 billion more per year than is spent now. This is 0.1% of world income. World military spending is US$780 billion per year. US$50 billion is spent on cigarettes in Europe every year.

Fair trade

Fair trade guarantees higher, more stable prices for third world producers. Look out for products with a Fairtrade Mark.

Debt campaigning

Find out more about Cafod's campaign on their website.

Environment

Look out for local Agenda 21 activities. The next UN environment summit will take place in 2002.

Gender

When we measure poverty we find differences between the level experienced by men or boys, and women or girls. Women may be disadvantaged through lack of access to education; in some countries they are not allowed to own or inherit land; they are less well paid than men.

Environment

A child born in an industrialised country will add more to pollution over his or her lifetime than 30-50 children born in the third world. However, the third world child is likely to experience the consequences of pollution in a much more devastating way. For example, annual carbon dioxide emissions have quadrupled in the last 50 years. This contributes to global warming, leading to devastating changes in weather patterns. Bangladesh could lose up to 17% of its land area as water levels rise.

Human Development Report 1998

■ The above information is from CAFOD's web site which can be found at www.cafod.org.uk

© CAFOD

Understanding poverty

Information from the World Bank

What is poverty?

Poverty is hunger. Poverty is lack of shelter. Poverty is being sick and not being able to see a doctor. Poverty is not being able to go to school and not knowing how to read. Poverty is not having a job, is fear for the future, living one day at a time. Poverty is losing a child to illness brought about by unclean water. Poverty is powerlessness, lack of representation and freedom.

Poverty has many faces, changing from place to place and across time, and has been described in many ways. Most often, poverty is a situation people want to escape. So poverty is a call to action – for the poor and the wealthy alike – a call to change the world so that many more may have enough to eat, adequate shelter, access to education and health, protection from violence, and a voice in what happens in their communities.

Dimensions of poverty

To know what helps to alleviate poverty, what works and what does not, what changes over time, poverty has to be defined, measured, and studied – and even lived. As poverty has many dimensions, it has to be looked at through a variety of indicators – levels of income and consumption, social indicators, and now increasingly indicators of vulnerability to risks and of socio-political access.

So far, much more work has been done using consumption or income-based measures of poverty. But some work has been done on non-income dimensions of poverty, most notably in the *Human Development Report* prepared annually by the United Nations Development Programme, and new work is under way in preparation for the *World Development Report on Poverty and Development.*

Poverty is not having a job, is fear for the future, living one day at a time. Poverty is powerlessness, lack of representation and freedom

---

Measuring poverty

Measuring poverty at the country level

The most commonly used way to measure poverty is based on incomes or consumption levels. A person is considered poor if his or her consumption or income level falls below some minimum level necessary to meet basic needs. This minimum level is usually called the 'poverty line'. What is necessary to satisfy basic needs varies across time and societies. Therefore, poverty lines vary in time and place, and each country uses lines which are appropriate to its level of development, societal norms and values.

Information on consumption and income is obtained through sample surveys, during which households are asked to answer detailed questions on their spending habits and sources of income. Such surveys are conducted more or less regularly in most countries. These sample survey data collection methods are increasingly being complemented by participatory methods, where people are asked what their basic needs are and what poverty means for them. Interestingly, new research shows a high degree of concordance between poverty lines based on objective and subjective assessments of needs.

Measuring poverty at the global level

When estimating poverty worldwide, the same reference poverty line has to be used, and expressed in a common unit across countries. Therefore, for the purpose of global aggregation and comparison, the World Bank uses reference lines set at $1 and $2 per day in 1993 Purchasing Power Parity (PPP) terms (where PPPs measure the relative purchasing power of currencies across countries). It has been estimated that in 1998 1.2 billion people worldwide had consumption levels below $1 a day – 24 per cent of the population of the developing world – and 2.8 billion lived on less than $2 a day. These figures are lower than earlier estimates, indicating that some progress has taken place, but they still remain too high in terms of human suffering, and much more remains to be done. And it should be

emphasised that for analysis of poverty in a particular country, the World Bank always uses poverty line(s) based on norms for that society.

Because of the time involved in collecting and processing the household survey data upon which these figures are based, and because of the complexities of the estimation exercise, these figures appear with a lag, and are updated only every three years.

New directions in poverty measurement

While much progress has been made in measuring and analysing income poverty, efforts are needed to measure and study the many other dimensions of poverty. Work on non-income dimensions of poverty – defining indicators where needed, gathering data, assessing trends – is under way in preparation for the *World Development Report on Poverty and Development*, which will be published in September 2000. The agenda includes assembling comparable and high-quality social indicators for education, health, access to services and infrastructure. It also includes developing new indicators to track other dimensions – for example risk, vulnerability, social exclusion, access to social capital – as well as ways to compare a multi-dimensional conception of poverty, when it may not make sense to aggregate the various dimensions into one index.

In addition to expanding the range of indicators of poverty, work is needed to integrate data coming from sample surveys with information obtained through more participatory techniques, which usually offer rich insights into why programmes work or do not. Participatory approaches illustrate the nature of risk and vulnerability, how cultural factors and ethnicity interact and affect poverty, how social exclusion sets limits to people's participation in development, and how barriers to such participation can be removed. Again, work on integrating analyses of poverty based on sample surveys and on participatory techniques is under way in preparation for the WDR.

■ The above information is from the World Bank's web site which can be found at www.worldbank.org

© The World Bank

Hunger questions

Who is hungry?

How many?

If food was evenly distributed, each human being would have plenty to eat. However, between 750 and 800 million people throughout the world do not have enough to eat.

The number of people suffering from malnutrition has been decreasing over the last thirty years:

■ In 1970, there almost one billion were affected by hunger. In Developing Countries, one inhabitant in three did not get enough to eat.

■ In 1996, the 750 million people suffering from malnutrition represented one in six of the same population.

Where?

Three quarters of those suffering from malnutrition are from rural areas, and one quarter are city dwellers living in the shanty towns of big cities in poor countries. 550 million suffering from malnutrition live in Asia and 170 million in sub-Saharan Africa, the principal areas of malnutrition. The number malnourished has fallen worldwide, except for Africa where policies which are hostile to agriculture and particularly the frequency of conflicts striking the civilian populations explain the continuing extent of hunger:

■ although the African population represents less than 15% of the world's population, it has more than one quarter of the world's undernourished population.

■ of the 23 million refugees throughout the world, most of whom depend on food aid to survive, 40% are in Africa.

■ of the 30 million displaced people throughout the world (i.e. those who have had to leave their homes and their land, who have often lost everything and could not reach a border, thus being unable to benefit from international protection), one third are in Africa.

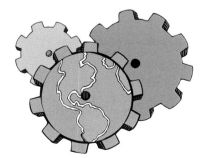

While the development of a country is almost always accompanied by a decrease in the number of victims of malnutrition, hunger has nonetheless reappeared in the West, as a result of poverty and exclusion. The same is true in Eastern Europe and in the former USSR, where the end of socialist regimes resulted in the collapse of collective agriculture which had formerly been protected by subsidies. Added to this, the acute vulnerability of elderly people, whose income has collapsed with the liberalisation of the economy, is clearly evident.

What is the difference between famine and malnutrition?

Although they both primarily affect those known as risk populations – children under five, pregnant and lactating women, the elderly and the sick – famine and malnutrition should not be considered the same, as they have different causes, different consequences and are not equally serious.

Famine is a state of acute hunger, with the total lack of food supplies for entire populations which will inevitably result in death if nothing is done to help them. Famine affects people whose only 'wrong' is to find themselves involved in conflicts where hunger is increasingly being used as a political weapon.

Somalia, Ethiopia, Liberia, Sierra Leone, Mozambique, Angola, South Sudan, Great Lakes regions – the famines in all these countries in the last two decades have been the result of violent conflicts, with thousands of refugees or displaced persons who are always the first victims of hunger.

Malnutrition, by comparison, is 'silent hunger'. It is possible to be malnourished without feeling hungry, if one's food intake is poorly balanced both in terms of quantity and quality and prevents normal activities. Although they do have food to eat, millions of human beings suffering from malnutrition are deprived of certain vitamins, minerals and substances which are vital for their development. Although malnutrition is a phenomenon which is widespread in underdeveloped countries, its consequences are not as dramatic as those of a famine. It can be combated by immediate curative and longer-term development programmes, aimed at increasing agricultural production and at improving health and eating habits.

Why Hunger?

A demographic problem?

No. There is no link between population density and the level of nutrition. It is not necessarily in the most densely populated countries that people suffer most from hunger. Java, in Indonesia, is densely populated but its population is well-fed, as it has a dynamic agriculture and high yields. Conversely, people are dying of hunger in vast, scarcely populated countries. It all depends on the incentives for agricultural production and on whether the economy is sufficiently diversified or going through a period of recession. It is not the number of human beings which counts, but the way they use the environment in which they live. Paradoxically, high population density has often led to agricultural innovations which have resulted in an increased yield and thus an improved nutritional status of populations.

A problem of distribution?

Yes. Hunger persists because it is not related to the problem of food availability, but of equal distribution. Even if there is excess food production in a country some populations do not have access to correct nutrition. This is the case in Brazil, which is, after all, one of the world's major exporters of cereals, or in India, which, although it is self-sufficient in terms of food at national level, has two and a half times as many malnourished children as the whole of sub-Saharan Africa (70 million).

A consequence of poverty?

Yes. Malnutrition primarily affects the poor:

■ because they do not produce sufficient food to meet their requirements,

■ because they are too poor to buy food,

■ because their training is insufficient to prevent them from making serious errors concerning nutrition, especially for their children – unsuitable food, abrupt weaning, diarrhoea which is either left untreated or not properly treated.

A political weapon?

Yes. Famine is no longer purely a result of natural disaster. The map of great famines exactly matches that of wars. In fact, climatic defects leading to droughts are often forecast months in advance – the world has ample time to prevent food shortages by despatching food to the most vulnerable populations. So today famines are no longer purely the result of natural disaster. They most frequently occur in situations of unrest where some parts of the population are denied access to food. The combination of war and climatic problems, the impossibility of delivering aid to victims, because these are blocked by people exploiting famine situations for financial gain, are all combinations of factors which explain famine.

Famines have become the preferred weapon in modern conflicts: they can be deliberately created, exposed, or even be denied.

Deliberately created famines

The dynamics behind these famines: Civilian populations are forced into towns where it is impossible to gather food from the fields and bring in their harvest, so they starve to death.

The 'usefulness' of artificially created famines:

■ they call in humanitarian aid which can then be hijacked by armed forces.

■ they acquire a political legitimacy by prioritising international recognition over access to victims.

Affected countries:

■ Angola, where insecurity and landmines are preventing civilians from returning to the fields for the harvest.

■ Liberia and Sierra Leone, where the different armed factions have mastered the art of using hunger to sustain the war effort.

■ The above information is from Action Against Hunger's web site which can be found at www.aahuk.org

© Action Against Hunger

100m more must survive on $1 a day

IMF and World Bank told to stop peddling discredited policies

By Charlotte Denny and Larry Elliott

More than 100m people in the world's poorest countries will be dragged below the basic subsistence level of a dollar a day by 2015 as they become ensnared in globalisation's poverty trap, the UN warned yesterday.

An in-depth study into the world's 49 least developed countries rejects claims that globalisation is good for the poor, arguing that the international trade and economic system is part of the problem, not the solution.

'The current form of globalisation is tightening rather than loosening the international poverty trap,' the study warns.

As markets become more entwined, the UN says the world economy is becoming increasingly polarised and the least developed countries are being left behind.

Shut out of more lucrative markets by western trade barriers, they depend on cash crops for survival, but the prices of their main export goods have crashed over the last two decades. Living standards in the least developed countries, which depend on basic commodities, are lower now than they were 30 years ago.

'International policy needs to give more attention to breaking the link between primary commodity dependence, pervasive extreme poverty and unsustainable external debt,' the UN says.

Simplistic calls for poor countries to open their markets will not help them escape the poverty trap, according to the study.

Trade's poverty trap

'Contrary to conventional wisdom, persistent poverty in poor countries is not due to insufficient trade liberalisation,' the study says. In fact in the poorest countries, trade accounts for just over 40% of GDP – higher than the average for rich countries.

'The problem for the least developed countries is not the level of integration with the world economy but rather the form of the integration,' the report says. 'For many LDCs external trade and finance relationships are an integral part of the poverty trap.'

Despite efforts by western donors to tackle the third world's loans burden, the poorest countries are still lumbered with unpayable debts. The 23 least developed countries have a debt burden which is unsustainable, according to the World Bank.

The UN says that servicing the debt overhang is swallowing official aid budgets. 'Aid disbursements have increasingly been allocated to ensure that official debts are serviced,' the study says.

'In this aid/debt service system, the development impact of aid is being undermined.'

Widespread poverty is itself contributing to economic stagnation. With most households earning barely enough to survive, there is no spare cash for the investment that might help countries break out of the poverty trap.

> *The study calculates that 307 million people live on less than a dollar a day, a number which is set to rise to 420 million over the next decade and a half*

'Low income leads to low savings, low savings lead to low investment and low investment leads to low productivity and low income.'

The UN says the number of people living in extreme poverty in the least developed countries is greater than had previously been thought. The study calculates that 307 million people live on less than a dollar a day, a number which is set to rise to 420 million over the next decade and a half.

The study underlines the scale of the challenge global leaders set themselves two years ago when they promised at the UN's millennium summit to halve the number of the world's population that live on less than a dollar a day by 2015.

None of the 49 least developed countries is on track to meet the poverty reduction target.

Although it warns that the extent of poverty has been underestimated, the study manages to strike an upbeat note, insisting that with better policies, rapid gains in living standards could be achieved. Poor countries should be allowed to abandon the economic adjustment programmes they were forced to adopt in the 1990s by the IMF and the World Bank.

Countries must 'shift from adjustment-orientated poverty reduction strategies to development-oriented poverty reduction strategies,' the study says.

It adds that widespread poverty in the least developed countries could be cut by two-thirds over the next 15 years, if the right policies were adopted.

■ *The Least Developed Countries Report, 2002: Escaping the Poverty Trap* is published by the UN Conference on Trade and Development.

Food crisis

Imagine trying to feed a family of 19 on scraps of food for 8 months and then running out of scraps. For many families in Malawi today this is a reality

Field workers for EveryChild, a leading children's international development charity, are seeing at first hand the devastating effects of the southern Africa food crisis which will leave over 14 million people in 7 countries across the region without food by the end of the year.

The Moyo family, from a village in the Engucwini district in Northern Malawi, have been surviving on maize husks since December last year. The husks are usually thrown away after the interior has been pounded to make 'Nsima', the staple diet. 3 weeks ago the family ran out of husks and have been surviving on handouts from neighbours and friends who are barely able to feed their own families. The Moyos have been identified by EveryChild project staff as being amongst the most vulnerable families and are now receiving World Food Programme food aid distributed by EveryChild as a supplement to their meagre rations.

Head of the family and widower Mrs Tassy Moyo, who is in her late 60s, has 2 sons, 3 daughters-in-law and 13 grandchildren living with her. She has already lost her husband and one of her sons, and one of the grandchildren is an orphan from her extended family. While her sons work on their small tobacco crop, their only source of income, which does not produce enough to sell in order to buy food for the whole family, the rest of the family look for 'Ganyu' (the local word for casual labour) for a plate of maize or a small bag of husks for a day's work. This is life in southern Africa: there is no social security, no hardship loans, the only coping mechanism for those in rural areas is for the whole community to share what little they have, which they do without question.

Mrs Moyo said: 'My sons do not have enough seeds to plant for next year, we are hoping to find work to buy enough seeds for next year's crop'

Helping children worldwide

Mrs Moyo has worked hard her entire life, and at her age she should be looking forward to slowing down and taking it easy; instead she has the worry of her entire family's future on her shoulders and that future is looking quite bleak.

In Malawi alone 3.2 million people (over a third of the total

---

This is life in southern Africa, there is no social security no hardship loans, the only coping mechanism for those in rural areas is for the whole community to share what little they have

---

population) are facing severe food shortages caused by 2 years of failed crops, adverse weather conditions, regional political instability and the catastrophic effect HIV/AIDS has had on the labour force. Next year doesn't look much better, with no seedlings to plant and the predicted devastating consequence El Nino will have on weather patterns affecting the region. Along with other international aid and development agencies, EveryChild are raising funds and organising emergency feeding and food security programmes and distributing seeds and fertiliser in the field for next year's crop in response to what has been described as the worst humanitarian crisis facing the world today.

Note
EveryChild have case studies, people in the field and spokespeople in the UK who are offering their services, knowledge and on-the-ground experience to the media in order to aid coverage of the crisis.

■ The above information is from EveryChild's web site which can be found at www.everychild.org.uk
© EveryChild

Trends in poverty over time

Information from the World Bank

Living standards have improved . . .
Living standards have risen dramatically over the last decades. Per capita private consumption growth in developing countries has averaged about 1.4 per cent a year between 1980 and 1990 and 2.4 per cent between 1990 and 1999. So millions have left behind the yoke of poverty and despair. But population in the developing world has grown rapidly – from 2.9 billion people in 1970 to 5.1 billion in 1999 – and many have been born into poverty.

The proportion of the developing world's population living in extreme economic poverty – defined as living on less than $1 per day (in 1993 dollars, adjusted to account for differences in purchasing power across countries) – has fallen from 28 per cent in 1987 to 23 per cent in 1998.

Substantial improvements in social indicators have accompanied growth in average incomes. Infant mortality rates have fallen from 107 per 1,000 live births in 1970 to 59 in 1999. On average, life expectancy has risen by four months each year since 1970. Growth in food production has substantially outpaced that of population. Governments report rapid progress in primary school enrolment. Adult literacy has also risen, from 53 percent in 1970 to 74

Trends in under-5 mortality						
Region	1970	1980	1990 (per 1,000)	1997	1998	Reduction 1990-1998
East Asia and Pacific	126	82	55	46	43	22%
Europe and Central Asia	n.a.	n.a.	34	29	26	24%
Latin America and Caribbean	123	78	49	41	38	24%
Middle East and North Africa	200	136	71	58	55	22%
South Asia	209	180	121	100	89	26%
Sub-Saharan Africa	222	188	155	153	151	3%
Developing countries	167	135	91	84	79	14%
OECD	26	14	9	6	6	30%

Source: World Bank Statistical Information Management and Analysis (SIMA) database

per cent in 1998. And gender disparities have narrowed, with the female-male difference in net enrolment rates decreasing from 11 per cent in 1980 to 5 per cent in 1997. The developing world today is healthier, wealthier, better fed, and better educated.

. . . but wide regional disparities persist.

While there has been great progress in alleviating poverty, it has been far from even, and the global picture masks large regional differences.

Poverty is rising rapidly in Europe and Central Asia, and continuing to rise in Sub-Saharan Africa. In Asia, where most of the world's poor live, the proportion in poverty has declined dramatically over the past two decades, but the recent crisis has slowed progress. And 4 in 10 households (over 500 million people) still remain in poverty in South Asia.

There are sharp regional differences also in a number of social indicators.

Most developing regions have seen infant and child mortality rates decline sharply. But South Asia's infant mortality rates today are about the same as East Asia's in the early 1970s, reflecting both poor progress in South Asia and favourable initial social conditions in East Asia. Sub-Saharan Africa's infant mortality rates are well above those in East

Asia some 30 years ago, and child mortality is rising because of the AIDS epidemic. On average, 151 of every 1,000 African children die before the age of five, and 92 in 1,000 before the age of one. Nine African countries have under-five mortality rates in excess of 200 (Angola, Burkina Faso, Guinea-Bissau, Malawi, Mali, Mozambique, Niger, Rwanda, and Sierra Leone).

Gross primary school enrolment rates have risen in all regions. But Sub-Saharan Africa's rates, having risen from 51 per cent of the eligible population in 1970 to 80 per cent by 1980, fell back to 78 in 1994, reflecting larger problems. Again, averages disguise wide country disparities. Nine countries in Africa have fewer than half their children enrolled in primary school (among them, Burkina Faso, Ethiopia, Mali, and Niger).

The extent of gender disparities in education, as measured by the male-female gap in the percentage of 6- to 14-year-olds in school, varies enormously across countries. Female disadvantage in education is large in Western and Central Africa, North Africa and South Asia. In several Latin American countries, instead, there is a female advantage.

■ The above information is from the World Bank's web site which can be found at www.worldbank.org
© The World Bank

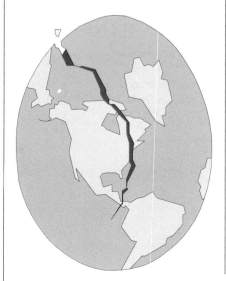

Leaders 'lack will to solve world poverty'

By Andy McSmith

Leaders of the world's richest nations were accused of lacking the will to tackle world poverty yesterday, at the end of a G8 summit that had raised expectations of a huge relief programme for Africa.

While Tony Blair described the promise yesterday of an extra billion dollars (£660 million) in debt relief to Africa's poorest nations as a 'significant uplift' for the continent, aid organisations caustically pointed out that the Group of Eight nations spent the same amount every day on subsidies to their own farmers.

Andrew Graham, a spokesman for Care, one of the world's largest development agencies, said: 'This will make for nice headlines, but it's not new money. It was announced three months ago. If the summit is to result in less poverty in Africa, the rich-country leaders need to commit more.'

He added: 'The battle against terrorism has shown us what governments can do when they are committed. It's only a question of will.'

Last night, Oxfam described the debt relief package as 'peanuts'. A Downing Street spokesman countered that the British charity's criticism was 'absurd'.

Speaking as the summit closed, Mr Blair said: 'This rightly will be remembered and known as the summit that devoted the lion's share of its attention to Africa.

'We are going to help Africa to help itself. This is not old-fashioned aid, it's a genuine partnership for the renewal of Africa.'

Mr Blair and others insisted that it was a significant step that the summit should spend a whole day discussing an African Action Plan in the presence of African leaders such as the Nigerian President, Olusegun Obasanjo, and South Africa's Thabo Mbeki.

Mr Obasanjo said afterwards that the African participants were 'satisfied' with what he described as a 'historic turning point' for Africa.

'If we have a good departure, the likelihood is that we will have a good arrival, and I can say we have definitely had a good departure,' Mr Obasanjo added.

Both Mr Blair and the Canadian prime minister, Jean Chrétien, who was hosting the summit, had committed themselves publicly to a crusade for Africa.

But they were up against a lack of enthusiasm from other G8 nations, including Japan, which has its own economic problems.

France and the United States, meanwhile, show no sign of wanting to end farm subsidies which effectively lock Third World producers out of the market.

There have also been criticisms of the huge costs of the annual G8 summits. The amount that Canada has spent on the two-day event exceeds that country's promise of extra aid for Africa, despite the fact that Canada's prime minister, like Mr Blair, has turned Africa into a personal crusade.

However, Mr Blair yesterday repeated his well-known opinion that world leaders must continue meeting, despite the growing problems of security from terrorist threats and anti-globalisation protests.

> 'This will make for nice headlines, but it's not new money. If the summit is to result in less poverty in Africa, the rich-country leaders need to commit more'

The debt relief plan, intended to cover the fall in world commodity prices, was the only new decision settled on yesterday by the G8 leaders.

The summit also confirmed 2005 as the target date for the worldwide elimination of polio, a particular African problem, and set out a plan for improving primary education in 18 countries throughout the world, 11 of them in Africa.

The heads of the G8 nations also agreed to set up a mechanism to check on the progress of an agreement struck earlier this year at Monterrey, in Mexico, to increase Third World aid by £8 billion a year.

At least half that money will go to Africa, if governments there can demonstrate that they are sufficiently well governed to qualify.

International contact groups of African and Western governments are to be set up to try to end the wars in the Congo, Sudan and Angola.

Children speak out

Mohammed

Millions of children in Ethiopia are sick of being poor. Lack of good food and sanitation mean the poorest families are plagued by illness. But if you're poor you can't afford to be sick. Treatment that in the UK might cost one or two hours' wages in prescription charges can cost over a month's wages in Ethiopia. Families are faced with stark choices – eat or get medical treatment

Baby Yassin is dangerously ill. He's burning up with fever and his frail 21-month-old body is covered in infected sores. He needs medical help urgently. But his family, who live in a remote rural area of Ethiopia's highlands, can't afford to take him to the doctor.

'We don't have anything to eat, let alone money for treatment,' explains Yassin's 16-year-old brother Mohammed.

To get proper medical help for Yassin the family would have to walk 12 kilometres to the nearest

government health centre. Officially, treatment is free for the poorest families. But many health centres are desperately short of essential drugs, and patients are sent to buy them at private pharmacies which charge two or three times the government prices.

Poverty – poor diet, hygiene and living conditions – are making Yassin's whole family sick. His mother has pneumonia and has been bedridden for three months. His father has a constant cough and is too weak to work.

Yassin's brother Mohammed is the main earner, but he's weak with hunger. 'Sometimes we go for two or three days without eating. I don't feel like I can walk now. I need to sit down.' To get treatment for Yassin and his mother, Mohammed would have to work constantly, and save all his wages for more than a month.

Yassin's family can only afford prayers to help him. But time is running out. Mohammed pleads for help from the Government to treat his seriously ill baby brother, Yassin. 'The Government has the power to do anything. It can provide relief and healthcare.'

In the last decade, the Ethiopian Government has significantly

---

Many health centres are desperately short of essential drugs, and patients are sent to buy them at private pharmacies which charge two or three times the government prices

---

Ana Catalina

Thirteen-year-old Ana Catalina Ixcajoc lives on the outskirts of Guatemala City. She works five days a week in a tortilla bakery run by her aunt, and earns about £1.70 a day. She uses the money to pay for her schooling in the evenings and on Saturdays

'I decided to work three months ago so I wouldn't have to ask my parents for money. I like it because it helps me study and buy things. But it gets very hot with the heat from the fire, and you can't go out into the cold air straight after working because it makes your head hurt.

'I like having something to do. It makes me feel calmer. And I want to get ahead in life. I don't want to just stay in the house. I managed to save 300 quetzals (about £25), which was enough to buy everything I needed for the school uniform – the material, buttons and socks.

'My grandparents have always begged me to study hard so I won't have to spend my whole life working the land like they had to. Not knowing how to read and write is like being blind. They're very proud of me now.

'What's missing around here is education for all children, so they can study and get a career instead of selling vegetables in the market. But they have to work because their parents haven't got the money to send them to school. The schools are charging very expensive fees. And you need a uniform, which many people can't afford to pay for.

'The problem is that many young people don't get an education. Many of the boys spend all day working in the fields and hang out in the streets at night shouting nasty words at the girls because they don't have anything better to do.'

Focus on aid

Despite 50 years of aid, almost half the world's people still live on less than £1.30 a day. In an increasingly interdependent world greater contact between people makes the widening gap between rich and poor appear more stark, and the need to tackle poverty more urgent

New goals for the new millennium

In November 2000, world leaders set out goals to halve the number of people living in poverty by 2015. To meet these 'Millennium Development Goals' governments in many rich countries are taking a fresh look at their aid budgets. The events of September 11th added weight to the need for more aid – more people will stay poor following the economic slowdown after September 11th. Rising poverty could be a threat to future peace and security. Anger and frustration is growing amongst the poor as they feel unable to share the wealth enjoyed by others. This could create a fertile ground for terrorism.

New promises

Since 1997, the UK government's aid budget has grown by 45%. Roughly half known as 'bilateral aid' goes directly to individual countries. The other half is 'multilateral', challenged through international bodies like the EU and the World Bank. More aid now flows through non-governmental organisations (NGOs) that act on behalf of donors and work with local people.

In March 2002, the EU and the USA announced an extra £8 billion a year of aid by 2006. But according to the World Bank, aid will need to double in order to achieve the Millennium Goals. And there are still only five MEDCs that spend

---

Anger and frustration is growing amongst the poor as they feel unable to share the wealth enjoyed by others

---

Millennium Development Goals

- Halve the number of people living on $1 per day
- Halve the number of people without clean water
- Primary school for all children
- Reduce infant mortality by two-thirds
- Stop and begin to reverse the spread of HIV/AIDS

more than the UN's minimum target of 0.7% of GNP on aid.

Strings

Quality as well as quantity of aid is important. A lot of aid is 'tied' so that the countries have to buy goods and services from the countries providing the funds. Aid is also used as a way of persuading poorer countries to become allies with their donors. For example, 70% of US aid is spent on American goods and services, and more than half goes to

middle income countries like Egypt. 'Tied' aid is often used inefficiently and does more to help the donor country than support those that need help.

Recognising these problems, the UK government is 'untying' aid spending from British businesses and is encouraging others to do the same, including the EU. This way, more UK aid can be used to help poorer people lead longer safer, and healthier lives. Improving health care is a top priority, particularly in fighting HIV/AIDS. Giving children the chance to go to school is another.

New partnerships

The UK government is also changing the way it distributes aid. Instead of spending it on one-off development projects, more aid goes directly to governments in poor countries. Local people should be involved too. By recognising people's right to decide for themselves how to improve their

Aid

Net official development assistance (ODA) from individual Development Assistance Committee (DAC) member countries to Least Developed Countries (LDCs) as a group.

Donor country	Percentage of 2000 GNI (Gross National Income)	Millions of dollars 2000	Change from 1990 to 2000
Denmark	0.34	537	16.2%
Norway	0.27	424	-20.3%
Luxembourg	0.25	45	350.0%
Sweden	0.24	528	-31.9%
Netherlands	0.21	793	-4.9%
Ireland	0.14	113	438.1%
Portugal	0.11	118	18.0%
Switzerland	0.10	269	-17.2%
United Kingdom	0.10	1,406	68.6%
Belgium	0.09	213	-42.0%
Finland	0.09	109	-65.6%
France	0.09	1,141	-50.1%
Germany	0.06	1,206	-31.8%
New Zealand	0.06	27	50.0%
Australia	0.06	211	23.4%
Austria	0.05	102	-7.3%
Total	**0.05**	**12,211**	**-19.7%**

Source: UNCTAD secretariat calculations based on OECD, Development Co-operation Report, various issues and International Development Statistics 2001, CD-ROM. The Least Developed Countries Report, UN

quality of life, aid is much more likely to have a lasting, sustainable impact. In return, governments have to draw up their own master plans called 'poverty reduction strategies' to co-ordinate different kinds of aid and to justify how the aid will help the poor. But some say that countries have to follow the instructions of their lenders.

Barriers to development

Despite more and better aid, rich countries are still giving with one hand and taking more with the other. One way is through debt. Every day, sub-Saharan Africa spends £26 million on paying back debts to governments and banks in MEDCs. Although 26 countries now qualify for debt relief, half of these still spend more on debt repayments than on health care. Critics claim that debt cancellation is small change compared to other spending plans. For instance, the US government will spend over £900 billion extra on defence over the next five years, twice

as much as the combined debt of the poorest 52 countries.

Unfair trade

International trade rules make the situation worse. The EU has removed tariffs on goods from the poorest countries, yet tariffs elsewhere artificially raise the prices of goods from the developing world. Meanwhile, European farmers receive subsidies through the EU's Common Agricultural Policy (CAP). Although CAP subsidies may be cut in 2003, the US government has announced an 80% increase in their farm subsidies, the equivalent of over

£20,000 for every American farmer. Subsidies allow farmers to produce more and sell it cheaper, so by dumping cheaper surplus food on developing world markets poorer farmers have little chance of competing.

Rising poverty should concern everyone, and recent changes that channel more aid towards fighting poverty are a step in the right direction. Meanwhile more people are demanding a fairer playing field in international trade.

■ Visit www.globaleye.org.uk to find out more about types of aid, which countries meet the UN's 0.7% target, and which countries receive the most aid from the UK, USA and elsewhere.

■ The above information is an extract from *Global Eye* (www.globaleye.org.uk), Issue 19 – a magazine about world development published by Worldaware (www.worldaware.org.uk).

© *Worldaware*

A little goes a long way

Their money – it's not a handout but a hand up

Not too many people think of 'the poor' as entre-preneurial, hard-working people with plans to build a better future for themselves and their families.

But that's exactly what Altab Hossine and his wife, Rubi Begum, are. They own and run three small businesses, all made possible by partnership with World Vision.

'Before World Vision, I felt things were hopeless, and I wondered about the future of my children,' says Rubi.

Altab had similar thoughts: 'I pulled a rented rickshaw and all I earnt I had to spend each day just for my family to survive.'

Pulling a rickshaw is tough work. It's hot, physically demanding, and business is uncertain.

Altab and Rubi were among the poorest people in their community.

They received a loan of 2000 Taka (£23) from World Vision to buy a second-hand rickshaw. This meant there was no rent to pay and gave Altab the freedom to work longer hours, and so earn more.

In just one year, Altab and Rubi paid off their loan and saved enough to buy another rickshaw, which they rent out. Since then, they've made enough profit to buy five rickshaws, and a 'van'. A 'van' in Bangladesh is the equivalent of a pickup truck, except it has pedals! It's a rickshaw that, instead of a seat, has a small wooden platform about a metre square.

Altab and Rubi weren't content to stop there. With the money they saved, they invested in a water-filter business. Altab delivers the water-filters using his van.

The future looks bright for Altab's family. He shared his dream with us:

'We will buy a piece of land and build a house. This is a good place. This is my home and now I want to buy land here. We will have a latrine, and a garden.'

The future for Altab's family has been transformed through his hard work, his determination and a little help from his partnership with World Vision.

■ The above information is an extract from *Insight*, the magazine produced by World Vision. See page 41 for their address details. © *World Vision UK 2002*

Cows are better off than half the world

The growing chasm between rich and poor is threatening global security

Charlotte Denny

For half the world's population the brutal reality is this: you'd be better off as a cow. The average European cow receives $2.20 (£1.40) a day from the taxpayer in subsidies and other aid. Meanwhile, 2.8 billion people in developing countries around the world live on less than $2 a day.

The facts of global inequality are truly staggering. The richest 25 million Americans have an income equal to that of almost 2 billion people, while the assets of the world's three richest men, even after the recent fall in the value of stock markets, is greater than the combined income of the world's least developed countries.

Or consider this: the living standards of Sierra Leone, ranked bottom of the United Nations' human development index, are roughly equivalent to those in the west 600 years ago. Average income per head stands at only $130 a year – less than the $1-a-day level that the World Bank regards as subsistence level.

The impact of such extreme poverty is devastating. The average Sierre Leonian can expect to live until age 37, a life expectancy level not witnessed in the west since the industrial revolution. Three in every 10 children die before their fifth birthday in Sierra Leone, while infant mortality rates are higher than in England in 1820.

Two centuries ago, income per head in Britain, the world's richest country at the time, was three times higher than that of Africa, then the planet's poorest region. Today, the world's richest country, Switzerland, enjoys per capita income nearly 80 times higher than the world's poorest region, south Asia.

One World Bank economist has warned that as television and cinema bring home to the poor the gap between their lives and the west, the rich may have to lock themselves in gated enclaves to keep out the dispossessed and angry masses.

Grinding poverty is propelling migration, driving the best and brightest from the developing world to seek better opportunities elsewhere. Borders in the west are being sealed to economic migrants, with the result that the trafficking of people has become a more lucrative trade than drug smuggling.

Two years ago at the UN millennium summit, world leaders set themselves the task of halving global poverty over the next 15 years. They promised to eradicate hunger, reduce under-five mortality by two-thirds and get every child of primary school age into a classroom.

The cost of meeting these goals is estimated at between $40bn and $60bn on top of current aid spending – about a sixth of what the west currently spends on subsidising its farmers.

In its most recent assessment of the progress towards the goals set at the summit, the UN warned that 33 countries, totalling a quarter of the world's population, are likely to miss half these targets. Most such countries are in Africa. If living standards in the poorest states continue to rise at the current snail's pace, the UN estimates that it will take 130 years to rid the world of hunger.

Extraordinary efforts will be needed to get sub-Saharan Africa back on track, the UN says. Even to achieve just the target of halving poverty would require growth of almost 4% in income per head over the next 15 years, a heroic task for many sub-Saharan countries where living standards are now lower than they were 30 years ago.

But the task, while difficult, is not impossible. The proportion of the world's poor living in absolute poverty has fallen from 24% in 1990 to 20% today, because of rapid growth in east Asia.

In 1960, Senegal and South Korea had a GDP per head of $230. By 2000, South Korea had a per capita GDP of $8,910, even after the setback of the Asian economic crisis. Living standards in Senegal, however, had barely improved, with GDP per head at $260.

Fifty years ago, South Korea's main export was human hair; today it is a hi-tech leader supplying components for America's computer industry. Massive state support for the silicon chip industry in the 1970s gave the country a competitive edge which paid dividends in the 1980s and 1990s when chips became the building blocks of the hi-tech revolution.

Africa faces a hard task following Asia's success. Blighted by debt, conflict and unfavourable geography, it faces an unequal struggle in the current world system. Moreover, while South Korea was allowed to protect its infant industries from being overwhelmed by more mature competitors, Africa is being required to open up its markets by the International Monetary Fund and the World Bank.

The chances of Senegal following in South Korea's footsteps seem increasingly slender as rich countries continue to pull the development ladder up behind them.

But as globalisation leads to greater interdependence, tackling poverty is becoming a political as well as a moral imperative. A more just world would also be a more stable one.

Trade: what we're calling for and why

Information from Christian Aid

The Trade Justice campaign calls on world leaders to rewrite the international rules and practices that govern trade, with poverty reduction and environmental protection recognised as their highest priorities.

This means poor countries need rules that guarantee them:

- the right to help their vulnerable people and traders
- the right to sell their goods in rich countries
- assistance to regulate transnational corporations.

Time for a fairer world

Inequality is now beyond a scandal. Every 8 seconds a child dies of hunger while a short journey away 3 people control more wealth than the 600 million who live in the world's poorest countries. In today's world, millions of people struggle to survive each day on less than $1 while many companies and individuals command more wealth than entire nations.

Inspired by South African theologians, many Christians speak of *Kairos* – a moment of grace and opportunity, a time when God issues a challenge to decisive action. And all people campaigning for trade justice, whatever their faith and background, believe it is time for a fairer world – for all our sakes.

Why campaign on trade?

Many of us have already experienced our power to challenge the causes of mass poverty in the campaign to cancel poor countries' debts. We must continue to insist that these unpayable debts are cancelled in full. They are a scandal. But we must not stop there. It is even more fundamentally wrong that people and nations are so poor they are forced into debt in the first place. Changing this means challenging the basic causes of poverty. And that means transforming the way we trade.

> *'As we enter a new millennium, we must make trade work for the poor.'*
> Kofi Annan, UN Secretary General

- Poor countries account for only 0.4 per cent of world trade. Since 1980 their share has halved.
- The United Nations estimate that unfair trade rules deny poor countries $700 billion every year.
- Less than 0.01 per cent of this could save the sight of 30 million people in the developing world.
- Many poor countries are allowing international companies to exploit their workers and their environment in order to entice them to invest there.
- Income per person in the poorest countries in Africa has fallen by a quarter in the last 20 years.

Trade should be a means by which poor people can lift themselves out of poverty, not the prison that locks them into it. Trade should be environmentally sustainable – ensuring the planet is preserved for the benefit of all.

In today's world, millions of people struggle to survive each day on less than $1 while many companies and individuals command more wealth than entire nations

---

Trade can be this positive force – if the international rules and practices that govern it are changed. At the moment, they are unfairly biased in favour of the richest nations and companies.

The Trade Justice Movement – a broad alliance of people and organisations – has formed to campaign for these rules to be rewritten, this time with poverty reduction and environmental protection as their highest priority. That way, the formidable power of trade can be harnessed to create a fairer, safer world for all.

The Trade Justice campaign says . . .

In such an unbalanced world, it is morally wrong to expect the poorest to compete on equal terms with wealthy and well-established international traders. If we do, then millions of people will be unable to earn enough to survive – let alone enough to enjoy life and make their contribution to the world.

In these circumstances, even stopping the rules favouring the rich and achieving a level playing field will not be enough. The international rules and practices that govern trade must give the weakest and most vulnerable special help until they are strong enough to compete without it. Without these measures those in the strongest position will continue to win most often; the gap between rich and poor will continue to grow and the injustice, inefficiency and instability of our world will get worse.

The special help that poor countries need boils down to three things:

1. Their governments need to be allowed to support and protect their vulnerable traders and people.
2. Their traders need to be allowed to sell the things they produce in the markets of rich countries.
3. Their governments need help to regulate the activities of large transnational companies.

How much difference could this campaign make?

Ultimately, it could change the world for the better beyond all recognition. Through the campaign to cancel poor countries' debts we won a commitment to cancel $100 billion worth of debt. For the world's richest governments, this is small change and they must still do more. But for campaigners around the world it is a huge victory.

- For millions of children it means the difference between receiving an education, or facing the struggle for survival without one. For millions of sick people, it means receiving health care rather than being left untreated.
- Through the generosity of those who support it, Christian Aid is able to give millions of pounds each year to help poor people in poor countries.

If Christian Aid had always been giving at its current rate, in order to give $100 billion it would need to have started around the time of Christ's crucifixion.

So in comparison, how important is the Trade Justice campaign? Based on estimates by the United Nations, changing the international rules and practices that govern trade could result in an extra $100 billion for poor countries – every 8 weeks!

Who is the campaign directed at?

World leaders. In particular, the campaign targets those with the greatest power – and therefore the greatest responsibility. This essentially means the Heads of Government and Trade Ministers of the world's richest nations.

'It wouldn't cost much to change the rules of trade so that poor countries can work their way out of poverty. But the world's leaders won't act unless they hear enough people telling them. And every day they fail to act, thousands of people die because they can't afford the basics of survival.'   Bono, U2

A moral issue, not an economic one!

You do not need to know everything about trade to be a trade justice campaigner. No one must feel they

should remain silent because they do not understand the complex economic issues that surround trade. Actually, there are so many trade rules that no one in the world understands them all!

Detailed trade issues can and should be debated by those interested in or responsible for them. But it is the responsibility of all of us to determine the morality upon which the economic debate is based. Essentially this campaign poses basic moral questions.

- Should poor countries have to follow trade policies laid down for them by an international community dominated by the rich, or should they be allowed the freedom to choose policies they believe will reduce poverty?
- When lives depend on the outcome, should weak and strong compete on equal terms?

The world has reached a fork in the road. A *Kairos* moment. Unless we act to change direction, we are headed down the path towards ever greater inequality and ever more dangerous instability. That path ultimately holds little hope for any of us. The other path leads to a fairer world and a hopeful future.

Just as the world has a choice to make, so does each one of us. We can choose to stay silent and allow the world to continue on its current course. Or we can choose to campaign.

■ The above information is from Christian Aid's web site which can be found at www.christianaid.org.uk
© *Christian Aid*

Debt relief works

New research

A new report from Jubilee Research at the New Economics Foundation reveals the difference debt relief is making in some of the world's poorest countries, and argues for further resources to be released.

The report *Relief Works: African proposals for debt cancellation – and why debt relief works* examines public spending in 10 African countries which have benefited from debt cancellation. It reveals that total spending on education in these countries has increased, and is now twice the amount being paid to foreign creditors.

The story is similar with spending on health, which has risen by 70 per cent since before debt relief, and is now one-third higher than spending on debt repayments. And contrary to the views of sceptics, debt relief is not being used to fuel military expenditure.

The report presents these clear indications of the positive difference that debt cancellation can make as the strongest argument there is in favour of further debt relief for the world's poorest countries.

Mary Bradford, Senior Campaigns Officer at Christian Aid, said, 'This is a really welcome report from our partners at Jubilee Research. It shows that our campaigning does make a difference to the world's poorest people and is such a strong argument in favour of further debt cancellation.'

■ The above information is from Christian Aid's web site which can be found at www.christianaid.org.uk

© *Christian Aid*

- No UK government has ever agreed an official definition of poverty, though the government does compile measurements of low incomes in the UK. (p. 1)

- The number of long-term workless households has been consistently above 2 million since 1995 and shows no signs of falling. (p. 2)

- A fifth of the poorest households did not have any type of bank/building society account in 2000/01, largely unchanged from 5 years previously. (p. 3)

- The proportion of children who are living in poverty has grown from 1 in 10 in 1979 to 1 in 3 in 1998. (p. 4)

- While poor people in Britain are not as materially poor as people in the South, their poverty is certainly real. It exists in lack of access to what is generally regarded as a reasonable standard and quality of life in the UK. (p. 5)

- In many of the world's poorest countries children under the age of 15 make up over 40 per cent of the population. (p. 5)

- There are two main approaches to measuring poverty. One sees poverty in absolute terms and tends to emphasis basic physical needs and discount social and cultural norms. The other sees poverty relatively, in terms of generally accepted standards of living in a particular society. (p. 7)

- The 10% of households in the top income bracket spent nearly seven times as much as the 10% with the lowest incomes. (p. 12)

- 'Teenage mothers are amongst the poorest and most vulnerable people in the UK.' (p. 13)

- More than one in ten older people find it 'difficult' or 'very difficult' to manage on their current incomes. (p. 14)

- Over 45% of women have a gross individual income of less than £100 a week, compared to just over 20% of men. (p. 15)

- 4.7 million women earn less than £5 an hour – 43% of all women employees. (p. 15)

- Child benefit rose by 26% in real terms since 1997, to £15.50 per week for the oldest child. (p. 18)

- The top three billionaires have assets greater than the combined GNP of all least developed countries and their 600 million people. (p. 21)

- The number of people suffering from malnutrition has been decreasing over the last thirty years. (p. 24)

- Today famines are no longer purely the result of natural disaster. They most frequently occur in situations of unrest where some parts of the population are denied access to food. (p. 25)

- Despite efforts by western donors to tackle the third world's loans burden, the poorest countries are still lumbered with unpayable debts. The 23 least developed countries have a debt burden which is unsustainable, according to the World Bank. (p. 26)

- The proportion of the developing world's population living in extreme economic poverty – defined as living on less than $1 per day (in 1993 dollars, adjusted to account for differences in purchasing power across countries) – has fallen from 28 per cent in 1987 to 23 per cent in 1998. (p. 28)

- Poverty is rising rapidly in Europe and Central Asia, and continuing to rise in Sub-Saharan Africa. (p. 28)

- Ethiopia now spends a fifth of its budget on health and education but this amounts to only about $1.50 per person. (p. 31)

- More than 100 million children are out of school because of poverty, discrimination or lack of resources. (p. 32)

- In March 2002, the EU and the USA announced an extra £8 billion a year of aid by 2006. But according to the World Bank, aid will need to double in order to achieve the Millennium Goals. (p. 35)

- Every day, sub-Saharan Africa spends £26 million on paying back debts to governments and banks in MEDCs. (p. 36)

- The US government will spend over £900 billion extra on defence over the next five years, twice as much as the combined debt of the poorest 52 countries. (Page 36)

- For half the world's population the brutal reality is this: you'd be better off as a cow. The average European cow receives $2.20 (£1.40) a day from the taxpayer in subsidies and other aid. Meanwhile, 2.8 billion people in developing countries around the world live on less than $2 a day. (p. 37)

- The United Nations estimate that unfair trade rules deny poor countries $700 billion every year. (p. 38)

- Less than 0.01 per cent of this could save the sight of 30 million people in the developing world. (Page 38)

- Income per person in the poorest countries in Africa has fallen by a quarter in the last 20 years. (p. 38)

ADDITIONAL RESOURCES

You might like to contact the following organisations for further information. Due to the increasing cost of postage, many organisations cannot respond to enquiries unless they receive a stamped, addressed envelope.

Action Against Hunger UK
Unit 7B
Larnaca Works
Grange Walk
London, SE1 3EW
Tel: 020 7394 6300
Fax: 020 77237 9960
E-mail: info@aahuk.org
Web site: www.aahuk.org

Barnardo's
Tanners Lane
Barkingside
Ilford
Essex, IG6 1QG
Tel: 020 8550 8822
Fax: 020 8551 6870
E-mail:
media.team@barnardos.org.uk
Web site: www.barnardos.org.uk

CAFOD – The Catholic Agency for Overseas Development
Romero Close
Stockwell Road
London, SW9 9TY
Tel: 020 7733 7900
Fax: 020 7274 9630
E-mail: hqcafod@cafod.org.uk
Web site: www.cafod.org.uk

Child Poverty Action Group (CPAG)
94 White Lion Street
London, N1 9PF
Tel: 020 7837 7979
Fax: 020 7837 6414
E-mail: staff@cpag.org.uk
Web site: www.cpag.org.uk

Christian Aid
35 Lower Marsh
Waterloo
London, SE1 7RT
Tel: 020 7620 4444
Fax: 020 7620 0719
E-mail: info@christian-aid.org
Web site: www.christian-aid.org.uk

End Child Poverty Coalition
10 Wakley Street
London, EC1V 7QE
Tel: 020 7843 1913/1914
Fax: 020 7278 9512
E-mail: info@ecpc.org.uk
Web site: www.ecpc.org.uk

EveryChild
4 Bath Place, Rivington Street
London, EC2A 3DR
Tel: 020 7749 2468
Fax: 020 7729 8339
E-mail: gen@everychild.org.uk
Web site: www.everychild.org.uk

Fawcett Society
5th Floor, 45 Beech Street
London, EC2Y 8AD
Tel: 020 7628 4441
Fax: 020 7628 2865
E-mail: fawset@gn.apc.org.uk
Web site: www.fawcettsociety.org.uk

HelpAge International (HAI)
PO Box 32832
London, N1 9ZN
Tel: 020 7278 7778
Fax: 020 7713 7993
E-mail: hai@helpage.org
Web site: www.helpage.org

Help the Aged
207-221 Pentonville Road
London, N1 9UZ
Tel: 020 7278 1114
Fax: 020 7278 1116
E-mail: info@helptheaged.org.uk
Web site: www.helptheaged.org.uk

NCH
85 Highbury Park
London, N5 1UD
Tel: 020 7704 7000
Fax: 020 7226 2537
Web site: www.nch.org.uk

New Policy Institute
109 Coppergate House
16 Brune Street
London, E1 7NJ
Tel: 020 7721 8421
Fax: 020 7721 8422
E-mail: info@npi.org.uk
Web site: www.npi.org.uk and
www.poverty.org.uk

Oxfam
Oxfam House
274 Banbury Road
Oxford, OX2 7DZ
Tel: 01865 311311
Fax: 01865 312600
E-mail: oxfam@oxfam.org.uk
Web site: www.oxfam.org.uk

Save the Children
17 Grove Lane, Camberwell
London, SE5 8RD
Tel: 020 7703 5400
Fax: 020 7703 2278
E-mail: enquiries@scfuk.org.uk
Web sites:
www.savethechildren.org.uk and
www.beatpoverty.org

Social Market Foundation
11 Tufton Street
London, SW1P 3QB
Tel: 020 7222 7060
Fax: 020 7222 3010
E-mail: info@smf.co.uk
Web site: www.smf.co.uk

UNICEF
Africa House, 64-78 Kingsway
London, WC2B 6NB
Help desk: 0870 606 3377
E-mail: helpdesk@unicef.org.uk
Web site: www.unicef.org.uk and
www.therightssite.org.uk

Worldaware
Echo House, Ullswater Crescent
Coulsdon, Surrey, CR5 2HR
Tel: 020 8763 2555
Fax: 020 8763 2888
E-mail: info@worldaware.org.uk
Web site: www.worldaware.org.uk
and www.globaleye.org.uk

The World Bank
1818 H Street, N.W.
Washington, D.C. 20433, USA
Tel: + 1 202 477 1234
Fax: + 1 202 477 6391
Web site: www.worldbank.org

World Vision UK
World Vision House
599 Avebury Boulevard
Milton Keynes, MK9 3PG
Tel: 01908 841000
Fax: 01908 841021
E-mail: info@worldvision.org.uk
Web site: www.worldvision.org.uk

YWCA
Clarendon House, 52 Cornmarket
Street, Oxford, OX1 3EJ
Tel: 01865 304200
Fax: 01865 204805
E-mail: info@ywca-gb.org.uk
Web site: www.ywca-gb.org.uk

INDEX

accidental deaths, and children 2
Africa
    debt relief programmes for 29, 36, 39
    food crisis in Malawi 27
    poverty in 28, 37
agricultural subsidies, and poverty in the developing
    world 36, 37
AIDS (Acquired Immune Deficiency Syndrome)
    in Africa 22, 27
    and development aid 35
Asia, poverty in 28, 37
asylum seekers, and child poverty 17-18

babies, low birthweight 2
burglaries, and low income households 3

child labour 32
child poverty
    children's own accounts of 9-10, 30-1, 32
    in the developing world 5, 30-2
        and education 21, 26, 30, 31, 32
        public attitudes to 20
    effects of 5
    in the UK 6, 9-10
        and asylum seekers 17-18
        defining and measuring 5, 6, 7
        and disabled children 10
        Government policies on 4, 6, 7, 10, 17-20
        and health 1
        public attitudes to 20
        statistics 2, 4, 6
consumption
    and the gap between rich and poor 12
    and the measurement of poverty 23
crime
    fear of 3, 14
    and low income households 3

deaths
    accidental deaths of children 2
    child deaths in the developing world 28
    infant mortality 4, 28
        reducing 35, 37
    premature deaths in the UK 1
debt
    and poverty in the developing world 21, 22, 26
        debt relief 29, 34, 39
developing countries
    aid to 35-6
    governments and 'poverty reduction strategies' 35-6
    poverty in
        causes of 21-2
        child poverty 5, 21
        measuring 21
        statistics 21
        and trade 21, 22, 26

    see also worldwide poverty
disabilities, and poverty 2
disabled children, and child poverty 10
diseases
    and poverty in the developing world 30, 31
    and poverty in the UK 1

economic growth
    in the developing world 37
    'trickle down' theory of 1
education
    in the developing world 21, 26, 30, 31, 32, 39
        and the Millennium Development Goals 35, 37
    poverty and educational attainment 2
elderly people
    and poverty
        in the developing world 33
        in former socialist regimes 24
        in the UK 3, 14, 15
employment
    Government policies on 19
    North-South gap in 11
    see also unemployment
Ethiopia, poverty in 30-1
ethnic minorities
    and poverty 3
        child poverty 17
        older people 14
European Union (EU)
    and aid to the developing world 35
    Common Agricultural Policy (CAP) 36

famine, and malnutrition 24-5
fathers, paternity leave for 16
food
    crisis in Malawi 27
    hunger and malnutrition 1, 22, 24-5
    and older people in the developing world 33
    weekly expenditure on 1, 12

G8 (Group of Eight) summits, and debt relief 29, 34
gender disparities
    in education 28
    in income 15
globalisation, and poverty 21, 26

health
    and poverty in the developing world 22, 30, 31
    and poverty in the UK 1, 2
HIV (human immunodeficiency virus)
    in Africa 22, 27
    and development aid 35
households
    expenditure patterns, gap between rich and poor 12
    incomes and financial decisions 15
    low income 3, 4

ACKNOWLEDGEMENTS

The publisher is grateful for permission to reproduce the following material.

While every care has been taken to trace and acknowledge copyright, the publisher tenders its apology for any accidental infringement or where copyright has proved untraceable. The publisher would be pleased to come to a suitable arrangement in any such case with the rightful owner.

Chapter One: Poverty in the UK

About poverty in the UK, © Oxfam, *Poverty key facts*, © New Policy Institute, *New website uncovers picture of UK poverty*, © Guardian Newspapers Limited 2002, *Poverty key facts*, © End Child Poverty Coalition, *What is child poverty?*, © The Save the Child Fund, *The child poverty league*, © UNICEF, *Child poverty indicators*, © Guardian Newspapers Limited 2002, *Holidays*, © UNICEF, *Poverty and social exclusion*, © NCH, *Poor measures?*, © Social Market Foundation, *The child poverty gap*, © UNICEF, *Listening to children*, © Children Poverty Action Group (CPAG), *Still Missing Out*, © Barnardo's, *North-south gap likely to widen, warn researchers*, © Guardian Newspapers Limited 2002, *Richest 10% spend seven times more than poorest*, © Guardian Newspapers Limited 2002, *Poverty and young motherhood*, © The YWCA of Great Britain, *Plight of pensioners*, © Help the Aged, *Ensuring that women live free from poverty*, © Fawcett Society, *Benefit will help fight child poverty*, © Guardian Newspapers Limited 2002, *It's all for the sake of the children*, © New Start, *'More needs to be done to tackle child poverty'*, © Guardian Newspapers Limited 2002, *Beating child poverty*, © MORI 2002, *Child poverty in different families*, © UNICEF.

Chapter Two: Worldwide Poverty

Poverty, © CAFOD, *1.2 billion people living in extreme poverty*, © paris21.org, *Understanding poverty*, © The World Bank, *Hunger questions*, © Action Against Hunger, *100m more must survive on $1 a day*, © Guardian Newspapers Limited 2002, *Food crisis*, © EveryChild, *Trends in poverty over time*, © The World Bank, *Leaders 'lack will to solve world poverty'*, © Telegraph Group Limited, London 2002, *Children speak out*, © The Save the Child Fund, *Income poverty*, © Save the Children, The World Bank, *Voices of young people . . .*, © UNICEF, *Dimensions of ageing*, © HelpAge International, *Debt campaign update*, © Christian Aid, *Focus on aid*, © Worldaware, *Aid*, © United Nations Conference on Trade and Development, *A little goes a long way*, © World Vision, *Cows are better off than half the world*, © Guardian Newspapers Limited 2002, *Trade: what we're calling for and why*, © Christian Aid, *Debt relief works*, © Christian Aid.

Photographs and illustrations:

Pages 1, 12, 21, 25, 27, 29, 32, 34: Simon Kneebone; pages 7, 9, 16: Bev Aisbett; pages 11, 14, 23, 30: Pumpkin House.

Craig Donnellan
Cambridge
January, 2003